CW00739630

UNIVERSE BY design

$E=mc^2$

An Explanation
of Cosmology
and Creation

Dr. Danny Faulkner

Master
Books

First Printing: October 2004

Copyright © 2004 by Master Books. All rights reserved. No part of this book may be used or reproduced in any manner whatsoever without written permission of the publisher, except in the case of brief quotations in articles and reviews.

Cover by Farewell Communications
Interior Design by Bryan Miller

For information write:
Master Books
P.O. Box 726
Green Forest, AR 72638

ISBN: 0-89051-415-1
Library of Congress Catalog Number: 2004106967

Printed in the United States of America

Photo and Illustration Credits

NASA: 5, 7, 20, 33, 44, 47, 54, 78, 79, 82, 83, 87, 88, 99, 110, 131
Bryan Miller: 9, 11, 12, 13, 16, 18, 21, 25, 27, 33, 37, 39, 40, 42, 60, 65, 68, 73, 89, 103, 111, 116, 119, 129
Corbis Stock Photography: 94, 108
Science Photo Library: 125

Dedication

To the late Roger L. St. Peter, one of the best friends and finest Christian men that I ever knew. This book would have been far better had he been able to help me with it.

Acknowledgements

I want to thank several people who read various versions of this book and offered many helpful suggestions. They are, in no particular order, Dr. Larry Vardiman, Mr. Steve Miller, Mr. Peter Mikula, Dr. John Morris, Dr Tom Greene, Dr. Ron Samec, Dr. Don DeYoung, Dr. John Hartnett, Mr. Andrew Kulikovsky, and Dr. Jason Lisle. I want to particularly thank John Morris and my good friend, Ron Samec, for encouraging me to write this book in the first place.

Table of Contents

INTRODUCTION

The first few chapters of the Bible describe what I, the author, believe to be the origin and early history of mankind, the earth, and the universe. Even a cursory reading of the Book of Genesis by anyone reasonably scientifically literate ought to result in awareness that the biblical and scientific stories of creation are markedly different. Not wanting to live in a fragmented world of the Bible on Sunday and science the rest of the week, most Christians develop some reconciliation of the two. Either this process results in a world view, or it is based upon an often tacit world view. For instance, one will usually attempt to reconcile the Bible to science or science to the Bible. It is important to understand what one believes in Genesis, because certain rules of biblical interpretation will be established here.

So, what assumptions do I make? I think that it is wrong to reconcile the Bible to science. In this book we will encounter many ideas that were once widely believed and thought beyond dispute, but were later shown to be wrong and were discarded. On the other hand, the Bible does not change. There are many today who interpret Genesis in terms of the latest scientific theories and even fads. If the history of science is any teacher, then we must conclude that many of these ideas eventually will be discarded. If we have staked out a position that Genesis teaches these ideas, then what is to become of Genesis when these ideas are abandoned? A great concern of mine is that many Christians have wedded the creation account of the Bible to the big-bang theory, the current scientific myth of the world's creation. In a hundred years will anyone believe the big bang? If not, then what is to become of Genesis if we have tied it to the big bang?

Attempts to reconcile the Bible to modern science include, but are not limited to, the following: theistic evolution, progressive creation, the gap theory, the day-age theory, and the framework hypothesis. Theistic evolution is the belief that biological evolution, as understood by most scientists today, was God's method of creation. Progressive creationists do not believe that different kinds of creatures evolved from other kinds, but instead think that God repeatedly intervened to instantaneously create new kinds of organisms throughout time. Extinctions then acted to eliminate many of those kinds of creatures. Thus theistic evolutionists and progressive creationists agree on when various organisms came into existence, but differ on how those organisms came into existence.

Both progressive creation and theistic evolution require vast periods of time, so some accommodation for the six days of the creation week must be made. The most common approach is the day-age theory, that is, that each of the days of the creation week were long periods of time. Some who reject both theistic evolution and progressive creation still feel compelled to allow for vast ages of millions or billions of years in the earth's past. In an attempt to permit this, the gap theory is the belief that there was a long period of time between the first and second verses of Genesis chapter 1. Then the six literal days of the creation week commenced with the second verse. The gap theory appealed to many people who wanted to interpret the Bible as literally as possible, but the gap theory has increasingly fallen onto hard times with the rise of modern creation science.

In recent years the framework hypothesis has made large inroads among conservative Christians who take the Bible seriously. The framework hypothesis is the idea that the first ten chapters of Genesis are poetry, not history. As such, those chapters have rich meaning, but do not reflect actual history. In this view, the Bible is silent on the how and when of the origin of the world, and so the believer is free to adopt whatever modern science has to say about these questions. All of these accommodations of Genesis to modern science have difficulties, a topic that will not be further developed here.[1]

What is the viewpoint of this book? The days of the creation week are best understood as literal days, not long periods of time. While the Bible does not tell us the date of creation, the strong implication is that the creation was only a few thousand years ago. There is a fairly complete chain of biblical chronologies from the creation to the time of Christ. Those chronologies add up to about 4,000 years. Adding the two millennia since the time of Christ, we determine an age of the world of about 6,000 years, though some understandings of the chronologies could stretch the age by nearly a thousand years. (Note that the precision of the Ussher chronology [4004 B.C. as the date of creation] is not possible.)

In any case, a faithful rendering of biblical chronologies will not allow for millions or billions of years for the age of the universe as demanded by modern science. Therefore, the approach that we take here is very different from the approach that nearly every other book on cosmology takes. At the time of the writing of this book, cosmologists generally estimate the age of the universe between 12 and 14 billion years. One particular study dated the age of the universe at 13.7 billion years, plus or minus 1%. We estimate the age at about 6,000 years. One would expect that this dramatic difference in estimated age must lead to tremendous differences in cosmology. Indeed, the standard big-bang model assumes a purely physical, natural origin

to the universe, while we assume that God created the world and revealed some of His process of creation in Genesis. That is, the origin of the universe was a supernatural event. This difference of opinion between theism and (at the very least practical) atheism is even more profound than the age issue.

WHAT IS COSMOLOGY?

The word *cosmology* comes from the Greek words *cosmos* and *logos*, which literally mean "world" and "word." As with the names of many sciences, *logos* has been generalized to mean "study of," while *cosmos* is generally understood to mean the universe. So the word *cosmology* means the "study of the universe" as a whole. More specifically, cosmology is the "study of the structure of the universe." A related word is *cosmogony*, which refers to the "study of the history of the universe." Today the word *cosmogony* is not used much, and much of what is called cosmology is technically cosmogony.

A cosmology is a particular theory or statement about how the universe or some part of the universe operates. For instance, the heliocentric theory, the idea that the sun is the center of the solar system, is a cosmology. The geocentric theory, that the earth is the center of the solar system, also is a cosmology. The idea that stars are very distant suns is a cosmology too. Another example of a cosmology is Immanuel Kant's island universe concept. At the beginning of the 20th century, many astronomers thought that our galaxy, the Milky Way, was the only galaxy. Thus, they often referred to the Milky Way as "the universe." Many faint patches of light seen through telescopes generally were thought to be clouds

Abell 1689 is one of the most massive galaxy clusters known.

of gas within our galaxy. However, much earlier Kant had suggested that many of these faint objects were other galaxies, each containing billions of stars. Since these "universes" were separated by huge gulfs of space, they were compared to islands. This theory was eventually proven to be correct, as we shall see.

The cosmologies that will be considered in this book will be those that are concerned with the structure of the universe as a whole. Since the mid-1960s there has been one dominant cosmology: the big bang. We will examine the historical developments and observations that led to the big-bang theory. We will discuss alternatives to the big-bang cosmology, such as the steady-state cosmology and the plasma universe. Besides the physical data, we will be very concerned with how well various cosmologies conform to biblical data. Creationists have recounted many problems with the big bang, and some of those problems

will be discussed here. However, it is important that creationists go beyond criticizing non-biblical or evolutionary cosmologies and develop our own positive models. Unfortunately, only meager progress to this end can be reported at this time, but avenues of possible research will be suggested.

In this introduction let us explore some more restricted cosmologies of the past. Cosmological ideas are as old as mankind. We have no idea what kind of cosmologies Adam may have had. Many people think that since Adam and his immediate descendents lived so long (in many cases nearly a millennium), the earliest people may have developed some amazing ideas and technology. There is no evidence, but it is possible that the antediluvian society may have produced some very sophisticated cosmologies. There are records of many primitive cosmologies[2] from around the world. Evolutionists usually conclude that these primitive cosmologies represent the original thoughts of ancient people. From the creation standpoint we would expect that what we refer to as primitive notions are actually declines from some earlier, more advanced ideas. Given that there is no direct evidence to support this creationary conjecture, let us start with some of the earliest known cosmologies.

ANCIENT COSMOLOGIES

Most primitive cosmologies start with some version of a flat earth with a sky suspended above it. The earth certainly appears flat locally, so this is not an unreasonable starting point. Most people today erroneously believe that the concept of a flat earth remained common until about the time of Christopher Columbus five centuries ago. Actually, belief in a spherical earth had been nearly universal among knowledgeable people for at least two millennia before the time of Christopher Columbus.

How did the ancients figure out that the earth was spherical? The ancient Greeks gave several arguments for the earth's sphericity, but we will only discuss the two better ones here. The ancient Greeks knew that a lunar eclipse is the shadow of the earth falling on the moon. They also noticed that the earth's shadow was always exactly circular in shape, regardless of the orientation of the earth at the time of the eclipse. If the earth were disk shaped, it would be round-but-flat and would cast circular shadows, but only when an eclipse occurred near midnight. For eclipses near sunrise or sunset the sun's rays would strike a flat earth obliquely, and would produce an elliptical shadow, but not a circular one. The only shape that always casts a

circular shadow is a sphere. Since all lunar eclipses showed that the earth's shadow is consistently circular, the Greeks concluded that the earth was spherical.

Another argument for the sphericity of the earth stemmed from the travel and exploration of the Mediterranean world by ancient Greek and other mariners. There was a major trading route between Greece and Egypt. The ancients noticed that stars that were barely visible in the southern sky in Egypt were not visible at all in Greece. Conversely, stars barely above the northern horizon in Greece were not visible in Egypt. This is due to the fact that the north celestial pole is at a higher altitude, or elevation in the sky, in Greece than in Egypt. This can only happen if Greece and Egypt are at different locations along a curved surface. Today we would say that Greece and Egypt are at different latitudes. Any travel north or south revealed the same phenomenon. A similar thing can be seen in the rising or setting times of the sun as one travels east or west. For instance, there is a three-hour difference between the east and west coasts of the United States. The ancients failed to notice this time difference in east-west motion, because they lacked the accurate clocks and rapid transportation that we have today.

More than 2,000 years ago, Eratosthenes, a Greek astronomer living in Alexandria, made use of this phenomenon to measure the size of the earth. Eratosthenes noticed that on the summer solstice near Aswan in modern day southern Egypt, no shadows of vertical objects were cast at noon. This is because the sun was directly overhead at noon on that date, and today we would say that this location is on the tropic of Cancer, the northern extent of the tropics. At noon on the same date (but obviously not the same year) Eratosthenes noticed that objects did cast shadows in Alexandria. The difference in the shadows at these two locations obviously meant that the two locations were on an arc, and thus the earth's surface is curved. Eratosthenes measured the lengths of the stick and its shadow in Alexandria and used trigonometry to find that the sun made an angle of 7° with the zenith, the point directly overhead. Seven degrees is about 1/50 of the circumference of a circle, so Eratosthenes knew that the circumference of the earth was 50 times the distance between the two cities. The answer that he got was within 1% of the correct value.

Sometimes creationists are accused of trying to introduce something akin to the flat earth. This plays upon the common misconception that until about 500 years ago nearly everyone believed in a flat earth and that the Church taught that the earth was flat. This is utter nonsense — the Church never taught that the earth was flat. Indeed, the high regard for Aristotle and other ancient Greeks by the medieval Church necessitated that ancient Greek ideas on the earth's shape be included in the teachings of the Church. This unfair attack upon creationists can be traced to the latter half of the 19th century in an attempt to discredit those in the Church who defied the acceptance of Darwinian evolution.[3]

As an aside, we should consider for a moment just what was involved in the medieval Church's adoption of ancient Greek thought. Augustine taught that at the fall of man in the Garden of Eden, it was man's will

and moral character that fell, not man's intellect. Man was still capable of perfect reason. The Church eventually saw in Aristotle and other Greek philosophers the best of what man's perfect intellect could produce. Arguing that all truth is God's truth, most of ancient Greek philosophy was adopted as dogma. This is most strange, considering that all ancient Greek philosophers were pagan. If they believed in any gods, they would have been polytheists. As we shall see later, ancient Greek philosophy taught evolution and an eternal universe. Both of these should have been anathema to the Church, but instead these two heretical ideas subtly slipped into western thought.

The most obvious astronomical motion in the sky is the daily rising and setting of the sun. It does not require much thought to eventually

Objects did cast shadows in Alexandria, Egypt, on the summer solstice.

With the sun directly overhead at noon, objects cast no shadows near Aswan, Egypt.

The difference in the shadows shows not only that the two locations are on an arc, but this phenomenon was used to calculate the size of the earth.

figure out that it is the same object that rises and sets each day. Next, one can reason that the sun spends the time at night passing under the earth to rise again in the east in the morning. From this it is easy to conclude that the sun is doing the moving. In other words, the geocentric theory is a good starting model. Ancient and primitive cultures concocted various explanations for the sun's motion. Most involved either the sun being a deity that traveled across the sky each day or an object that was ridden or propelled by a deity or other creature across the sky each day. Many cultures considered what the sun was doing as it traveled under the earth each night. All of these considerations amount to a cosmology.

Probably the next step was to notice that other objects in the sky shared in the east-to-west motion of the sun. The moon and most of the stars rise in the east and set in the west each day as well. To most people the sky appears to be round, like a sphere. Many Mediterranean cultures adopted the cosmology of the celestial sphere. This is the idea that the stars, moon, and sun are lights placed upon a hard, transparent sphere centered on the earth. Either the earth remained absolutely motionless as the sphere spun around the earth each day, or the celestial sphere remained motionless while the earth rotated each day. Either one of these options would be a geocentric model. Many people today assume that all ancient people believed that the earth did not spin, but this is not necessarily true. Once the ancients figured out the correct shape of the earth and had traveled over a few hundred miles, they recognized that at all points on the earth bodies are attracted by gravity toward the earth's center. Therefore there

was no danger in falling off the earth as it spun.

The question of strict geocentricity does not arise until motions taking quite a bit more than a single day are considered. From night to night the moon appears to move about 14° eastward with respect to the background stars. The length of time required for the moon to make one complete orbit with respect to the stars is 27⅓ days, or one sidereal month. So while the earth or celestial sphere is rapidly spinning each day, the moon is more slowly moving around the earth or celestial sphere once a month. Most ancient societies correctly deduced that this was the orbital period of the moon around the earth. Things got murkier as the motion of the sun was considered. Each day the sun moves about 1% eastward through the stars, taking one year to make one trek around the celestial sphere. The question is whether this is motion around the earth similar to that of the moon, or is it the motion of the earth around the sun? Both the geocentric and heliocentric cosmologies produce the same observed motion just described.

Most people today are under the incorrect impression that nearly all ancients believed that the sun orbited the earth because of certain philosophical biases. Actually, some ancients conducted an experiment to test which idea was true. They reasoned that if the earth orbited the sun, then the observed positions of stars on the celestial sphere ought to shift slightly as we view them from one side of the earth's orbit to the other. This effect is called parallax, which you can demonstrate by viewing your thumb held at arm's length with one eye and then the other eye. Your thumb will appear to shift back and forth with respect to background objects as you look with one eye and then the other. If we view nearby stars on one side of the earth's orbit and then the other side of the orbit six months later those stars will appear to change position. Parallax is caused by a change in viewing position along what is called a baseline. Surveyors use this principle all the time to measure the distance to points that are far away. The amount of parallax shift that we see depends upon the size of the baseline (the earth's orbit in the case of stars) and the distance to the object in question. For a given baseline, parallax will decrease with increasing distance to the object.

The ancients diligently searched for parallax, but did not find it. They could not appreciate the fact that stars are at incredible distances. The nearest star is about 275,000 times farther from us than the sun, so the total annual shift that the nearest star experiences is the equivalent of the apparent diameter of a dime viewed from about one and a half miles away! Being good

scientists, they rejected the heliocentric theory in favor of the geocentric cosmology. There were a few ancients that believed the heliocentric theory anyway, primarily upon the basis that the model was simpler, but they did so against the best evidence of the time.

The earliest mention of someone teaching the heliocentric model is Aristarchus of Samos (310-230? B.C.). Aristarchus used geometric arguments to measure the sizes of the moon and sun as well as their distances from the earth. He found that the moon was ⅓ the size of the earth and that the moon's distance was 10 times the diameter of the earth. Actually, the moon is ¼ the size of the earth and its distance is about 30 times the diameter of the earth. Aristarchus measured the sun as 7 times bigger than the earth and its distance was 200 times the diameter of the earth. The modern values are 109 and nearly 12,000. Still, these were remarkable measurements that were quoted for centuries

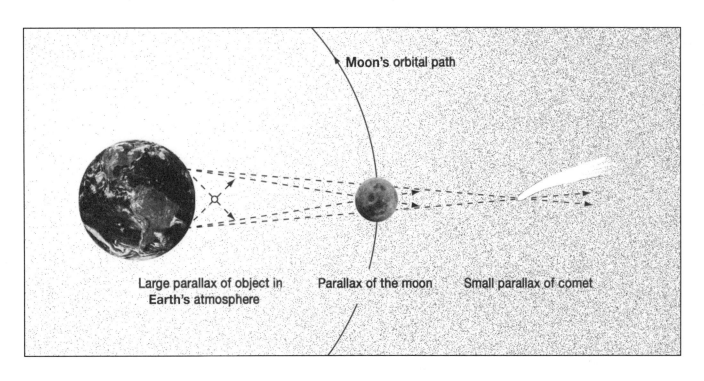

Parallax diagram

afterward. Since the sun is much larger than the earth, Aristarchus reasoned that it was more logical to conclude that the earth orbited the sun rather than the other way around. He explained the lack of parallax by concluding that the stars are very distant, which is, of course, correct.

HELIOCENTRIC AND GEOCENTRIC COSMOLOGIES

orbit the sun in nearly the same plane as the earth, the motions of the planets are always near the ecliptic.

While the planets moved close to the ecliptic, they seemed to follow erratic motions, which suggested the property of volition. Therefore, most ancient cultures conferred the status of deity upon the five planets, along with the sun and the moon. Our names for the five naked-eye planets come from the Roman pantheon: Mercury, Venus, Mars, Jupiter, and Saturn. With the

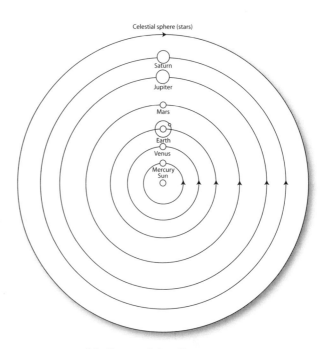

Geocentric diagram   Heliocentric diagram

The path that the sun appears to follow along the celestial sphere each year is called the ecliptic. The moon's orbit is inclined to the ecliptic a little more than five degrees. Of the few thousand stars visible to the naked eye, the ancient astronomers found that nearly all of them remained fixed on the celestial sphere. The only exceptions were five fairly bright stars that they called *wandering stars*. The Greek name meaning "wandering star" has come down to us as *planet*. Since all of the planets

discovery of Uranus, the first telescopic planet, in the eighteenth century, the practice of using Roman names was continued.

The motion of the planets among the stars is usually from west to east. This is called direct, or prograde, motion. However from time to time the direction reverses so that the planets travel westward. This motion is called indirect or retrograde motion. Soon afterward, the motion returns to direct. For Mars, Jupiter, and Saturn, which orbit the sun farther from it than the earth, retrograde motion occurs when they are nearly opposite the sun on the celestial sphere. Mercury and Venus orbit the sun closer than the earth does, and retrograde motion occurs when they move from being east of the sun in the evening sky to being west of the sun in the morning sky. Mars, Jupiter, and Saturn are called superior planets, while Mercury and Venus are called inferior planets.

How can retrograde motion be explained with the heliocentric and geocentric cosmologies? The heliocentric model can explain it very easily, as shown below. The orbital speeds of planets decrease with increasing distance from the sun. When the earth at the position marked "opposition" passes a superior planet, the faster motion of the earth causes the superior planet to appear to fall behind. This is retrograde motion. At other times the combined motion of the superior planet and the earth cause the planet to appear to

move in the prograde direction. When an inferior planet passes between the earth and the sun, it is the earth that is left behind, which causes the inferior planet to appear to move backward for a short while. The simplicity of this rather straightforward explanation has always been the primary argument in favor of the heliocentric theory.

How is retrograde motion explained in the geocentric theory? The most complete explanation comes from Ptolemy, a second-century Alexandrian astronomer. He wrote a compilation of all ancient astronomy in a book that has come down to us by the title *The Almagest*. Since no original or copies of earlier astronomy texts exist, most of what we know of ancient Greek astronomy comes from this source. Ptolemy could have simply had the planets move on erratic paths along the ecliptic, but this would have offered no predictive power. That is, one could not anticipate nor predict where planets would be at any time in the past or future. Furthermore, the

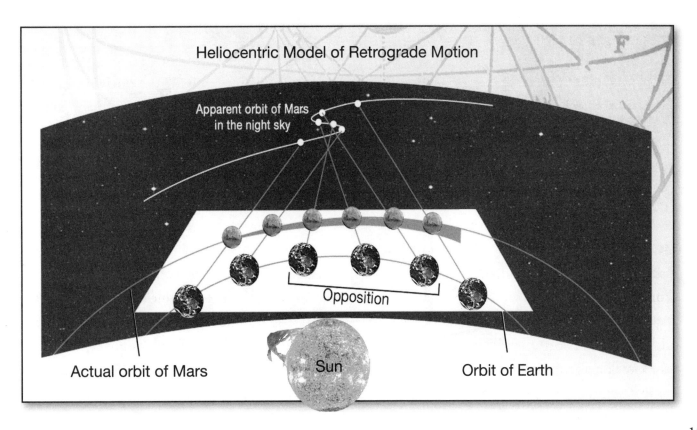

Heliocentric Model of Retrograde Motion

Apparent orbit of Mars in the night sky

Opposition

Actual orbit of Mars   Sun   Orbit of Earth

ancients reasoned that objects in the sky must follow perfect motion. The most perfect shape was the circle, and the most perfect motion was uniform. Therefore the ancient Greeks thought that planets must move uniformly along circular paths.

Ptolemy managed to explain retrograde motion by having each planet move upon two circular paths simultaneously. A planet moved along a smaller circle called an epicycle, while the epicycle moved around the earth along a larger circle called a deferent. A deferent went completely around the sky along the ecliptic. By adjusting the sizes of the circles and the rates of motion Ptolemy was able to reproduce direct and indirect motion of the planets pretty well. See the drawing on page 12 for an illustration of how this system works.

Further refinements allowed this system to reproduce planetary motions. For example, the planets do not follow simple back and forth motions when they retrograde. Because the orbits of the planets are slightly inclined to the ecliptic, the motions are flattened loops or flattened *s* shapes, depending upon at which portions of the orbits that retrograde motions occur. One can reproduce the looping motion by introducing smaller epicycles perpendicular to the other epicycles already discussed.

Ptolemy also found that he got better agreement when he placed the earth off-center of each deferent. This was an attempt to match the elliptical orbits of the planets, a fact elucidated by Johannes Kepler (1571-1630) as his first law of planetary motion in the early seventeenth century. The elliptical orbits of the planets are close enough to being circles that off-center

circles can approximate them. Kepler's second law dictates the rates at which planets move in their orbits. The result is that planets move most rapidly at perihelion, the point of closest approach to the sun, and most slowly at aphelion, the point of greatest distance from the sun. Ptolemy mimicked this by having each planet move at a uniform angular rate with respect to a point called the equant. The equant is collinear with the earth and the center of the deferent, opposite the center of the deferent from the earth, and equal distance from the center as the earth.

MEDIEVAL AND RENAISSANC COSMOLOGIES

The Ptolemaic system worked very well to predict planetary positions. By the time of Kepler, the errors between the model and reality were remarkably small. Further refinements (epicycles upon epicycles) could be and were added to improve the agreement. It is not clear if Ptolemy meant for his model to be taken as an absolute statement of how the universe really worked, or if it was merely a computational device. Whatever Ptolemy intended, by medieval times most people thought that was actually how the celestial world operated. Despite its ability to predict planetary positions, the Ptolemaic system was very cumbersome. It is said that when one late medieval monarch was instructed on the Ptolemaic cosmology, he commented that had he been present at the creation he could have offered God a few suggestions.

The complexity of the Ptolemaic cosmology

led to the pursuit of simpler explanations. In 1542, nearly one hundred and fifty years before Newton's work, Nicklaus Copernicus (1473-1543) published his book on the heliocentric cosmology. Copernicus is usually given credit for originating or at least establishing heliocentricity. This is not exactly true, because many others had previously believed in heliocentricity. Perhaps his greatest contribution was his development of the model. Using the heliocentric theory Copernicus found the correct orbital periods of the five planets then known. He also found the distances of the five planets from the sun. Copernicus expressed these distances in astronomical units (AU). One AU is the average distance between the earth and the sun. It would be many years before anyone would know the length of the AU in miles or kilometers, but this is not important, since often all that matters is the relative distances.

Neither of the sizes nor periods of the planets' orbits had been known previously. Kepler needed this information when he determined his third law of planetary motion in the early 16th century. By the time of Newton in the latter part of the 17th century, the geocentric theory was largely discarded in favor of the heliocentric theory. Direct evidence of the heliocentric option came about much later (aberration of starlight and parallax), but the debate was settled to the satisfaction of most people from the argument of simplicity. The principle of Occam's razor dictates that when confronted with two explanations that equally explain data, the simpler explanation is usually the correct one.

An alternate geocentric model should be mentioned. Tycho Brahe (1546-1601) was a famous Danish astronomer who made many very accurate measurements of stellar and planetary positions. The most remarkable part of his story is that he did this all without optical aid, because he died just a few short years before the invention of the telescope. Tycho realized how unwieldy the Ptolemaic cosmology was, but he was unwilling to totally let go of geocentricism, so he devised a sort of compromise cosmology. In the Tychonic model, the other planets orbit the sun, but the sun in turn orbits the earth. (See illustration on page 16.) This is not as different from the heliocentric model as it may seem at first. The Tychonic cosmology is mathematically a coordinate transformation between the earth and sun. There is a modern geocentric movement that embraces this system, and includes a small minority of recent creationists. The author of this monograph does not endorse this movement.[4]

Contrary to popular belief, Galileo Galilei (1564-1642) did not invent the telescope, though he was the first to put the telescope to astronomical use. With his telescope Galileo saw several things that challenged conventional cosmological thoughts of the day. Galileo saw mountains and craters on the moon and spots on the sun, though these bodies were supposed to be perfect and hence without blemish. He saw many thousands of stars too faint to be seen with the naked eye. At the time many thought that there were only 1,022 stars. This stems from the belief that all things worth knowing were known to the ancients and that Ptolemy had cataloged 1,022 stars. Of course Ptolemy had not claimed that he had cataloged all stars. Indeed, his catalog had more stars than those cataloged by earlier Greek astronomers; he had

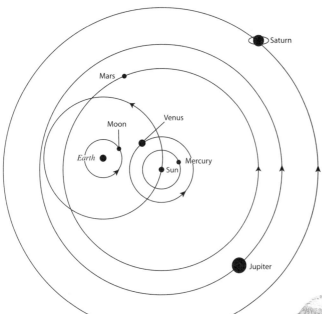

The Tychonic model

Tycho Brahe (1546-1601)

Scripture was rarely used in the prosecution. Instead, the works of Ptolemy were used. This is a strange approach if the question is really theological or religious in nature. We can understand this by recalling that during the middle ages all authority was collected in one place: the Church. The authority included religion, society, government, business, education, and science. A king could not rule, people could not marry or have businesses, and one could not attend school without the blessing of the Church. Most art and science was pursed with the patronage of the Church. Copernicus was a priest, and Galileo had much interaction with the Church. When Galileo and others proposed the heliocentric theory, it was not so much that they were challenging religious doctrine, as it was that they were challenging the science of the day. In other words, the conflict was over old science versus new science, not religion versus science. Given this reality, if one wishes to make a parallel between the Galileo episode of four hundred years ago to the rise of modern creation science, the creationists are to be identified with Galileo. Of course this is just the opposite of the usually intended parallel.

merely cataloged all the stars that he could easily identify. If the authorities had merely considered the words of God in His covenant with Abram recorded in Genesis 15:5 rather than relying upon a garbled understanding of Ptolemy's words, they would have realized that the stars are without number.

This episode concerning the number of stars sheds light upon what actually transpired when Galileo ran afoul of the Church on the issue of geocentrisim. The usual understanding today is that Galileo and others got into trouble for teaching heliocentricism because Church leaders thought that the Bible taught geocentricism.

What evidence did Galileo offer for the heliocentric theory? He discovered and named the four large satellites orbiting Jupiter. He realized that he had found four astronomical bodies that did not revolve around the earth, in contradiction to the dogma of the day. Defenders of geocentricism had claimed that if the earth moved, the moon would be left behind. That argument was undermined by the fact that in either the geocentric or heliocentric theories, Jupiter must move, yet its satellites managed to keep up with it. Galileo went on to suggest that Jupiter and its moons represented a sort of miniature solar system. Galileo also saw that Venus went through a complete range of phases, which it could only do if it orbited the sun. This ruled out the Ptolemaic cosmology, though it could not rule out the Tychonic model.

THE NATURE OF THE UNIVERSE

Given the important role that ancient Greek thought had upon the development of science, it is important to explore their ideas about the universe as a whole. The ancient Greeks thought that the universe was eternal, without beginning or end. This assumption became so deeply ingrained that it is difficult for us to totally understand why they believed it. One possibility is that they had a hard time conceiving of the beginning of the universe. If the universe had no beginning, then that nasty problem may be avoided. That sort of thinking has survived until today. The Greek gods were quite limited in their power – they were not much more than supermen. These gods were finite beings in a

transcendent universe. They were born at some time in the past, and presumably would eventually die. The Greeks could not comprehend a Creator that transcended the universe.

Another explanation why the Greeks believed in an eternal universe is that they were evolutionists. Contrary to popular misconception, evolution did not start with Charles Darwin's *Origin of Species* in 1859, or even with Lamarck a few decades earlier. The idea of spontaneous generation goes back at least to the ancient Greeks. They also realized that the universe tends to go from order to disorder. However they believed that vortices stirred portions of the universe in such a fashion that order occasionally arose. Variations on this theme still survive in Western thinking today.

Augustine, and later Thomas Aquinas, had a strong influence upon the development of the thinking of the Church and the philosophy of Western thought and science. Augustine brought in many ancient Greek ideas, and "Christianized" many of the formerly pagan concepts. While Augustine may have not believed in an eternal universe himself, his lead allowed that sort of idea to remain in vogue. The big-bang cosmology of the 20th century reintroduced the concept of the universe having a beginning. This was a clean break from the thinking since the 17th century when what we now know as science began to develop. Though some scientists in that interval may have believed in a recent origin of the earth, many of them undoubtedly believed in the eternality of the universe as a whole.

As an example of someone who believed in the eternality of the universe, consider Isaac Newton. After Newton devised his law of gravity, he realized that all of the matter in the universe attracted all the other matter. If the matter in the universe were finite in size, then there must be a center of mass. If the universe has a center of mass, then the center must be the point toward which all matter in the universe is attracted. If the universe is eternal, as Newton apparently believed, then there should have been ample time for all matter to be amalgamated at the center of mass. This obviously has not happened.

Newton solved this dilemma not by scrapping the eternality of the universe, but by hypothesizing that the universe was infinite in extent. He reasoned that if the universe extended infinitely in all directions, then there would be no center of mass. All matter would be equally attracted in all directions, so that there would be no collapse of all matter into a single heap. The eternality and infinite size of the universe persisted for two centuries. We shall see that with general relativity this option is not viable in the general case.

Isaac Newton

TOWARD MODERN COSMOLOGY

About a century after Newton, a clear picture of the structure of our galaxy, the Milky Way, began to emerge, largely through the work of the German-born English astronomer William Herschel (1738-1822). Herschel's model was called the grindstone model, because its distribution of stars was in a round, flat shape similar to a grindstone. This model placed the sun near the center of the Milky Way, not because of philosophical presuppositions, but because that was where the observational data placed it. In every direction along the plane of the Milky Way, Herschel's counts of stars at ever-fainter degrees of brightness changed as one would expect if the sun were at the center. It appeared that we were seeing to the edge of our galaxy in every direction.

In the early part of the 20th century, the American astronomer Harlow Shapley (1885-1972) found that the sun was not at the center of our galaxy. He did this by studying the distribution of globular star clusters. Shapley plotted the hundred or so globular clusters then known and found that while their common center was along the plane of the Milky Way, that center was many thousands of light years away from the sun. Since each globular cluster contains at least 50,000 stars, the globular star cluster system as a whole must have a mass many millions of times that of the sun. Shapley argued that it made more sense for the center of the globular cluster system to be the true center of the Milky Way rather than the sun.

Why star counts made it appear as if the sun were at the center of the galaxy remained a mystery for over a dozen years. In 1930 the existence of interstellar dust was discovered. Dust scatters, and thus dims, the light from stars. The amount of scattering is dependent upon the wavelength, or color, of the light. Blue light (shorter wavelength) is scattered more than red light (longer wavelength) so that the transmitted light is changed in color. Viewed through dust, a star appears fainter and redder than it ordinarily would, and if there is enough dust, the star may not be visible at all. This process is well understood, and astronomers routinely correct for this sort of thing today. There is so much dust in the plane of the galaxy that it is not possible to see completely to the edge, at least not in the visible part of the spectrum. We now recognize that obscuration by dust explains why star counts had incorrectly suggested that we were at the center of the Milky Way.

Shapley played a role in another cosmological debate, though this time on the losing side. In 1920 Shapley debated Heber Curtis in Washington, DC, in a program sponsored by the American Academy of Science. At question was Kant's island universe theory. Most astronomers had thought for a long time that the Milky Way was the only galaxy. In fact, the words galaxy and universe were used synonymously. Through the telescope thousands of faint patches of light can be seen. These were called nebulae (singular: nebula), after the Greek word for cloud, because these objects often appear cloudy. With larger telescopes some of the nebulae can be resolved into stars, and these became known as star clusters. However, most of the nebulae remained fuzzy.

Many of the nebulae had flat, circular or elliptical shapes that reminded Kant and others of Herschel's grindstone model. Therefore some thought that these might be very distant "universes" like the Milky Way. However, most astronomers interpreted the nebulae as clouds of gas within the Milky Way. The gas cloud theory remained more popular, largely because it fit so well with Laplace's nebular hypothesis. The nebular hypothesis was the idea that the solar system formed from a flat, rotating disk of gas. The modern theory of solar system formation is the intellectual descendent of the nebular hypothesis. A hundred years ago astronomers used the existence of "spiral nebulae" as proof of the nebular hypothesis.

In their debate Curtis argued for the island universe, while Shapley argued that the Milky Way was the sole galaxy. By all accounts Shapley won the debate, primarily because the data as then understood better supported his position. His victory was short-lived, because just four years later, in 1924, Edwin Hubble (1889-1953) confirmed the island universe theory. Hubble did this with very long photographic exposures of the Andromeda galaxy (M31) made with the Mt. Wilson 100-inch telescope, then the largest

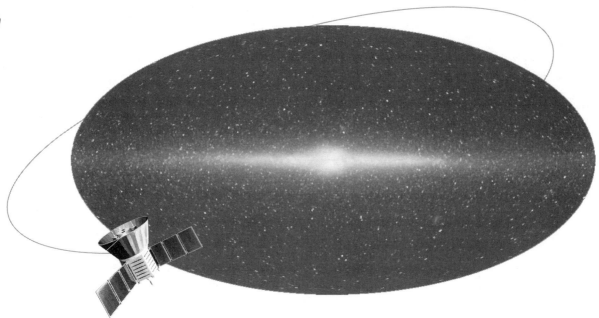

The above picture was taken by the COBE satellite
and shows the plane of our galaxy in infrared light.

telescope in the world. The photographs revealed faint individual stars in M31 that were identified as normally very bright giant stars. This could only be true if M31 were extremely far away (at the time, Hubble estimated its distance as nearly a million light years away), which placed M31 well outside of the Milky Way. Because M31 appeared to be the largest and brightest of the spiral or elliptical "nebulae," it followed that the others probably were even more distant galaxies, a conclusion that soon was confirmed.

Shapley's correct positioning of the sun off-center in our galaxy has been hailed as the continuance of the Copernican revolution. Just as Copernicus showed that the earth was not the center of the solar system, we are not even the center of the Milky Way. Hubble's confirmation of the island universe theory is often taken as the ultimate triumph of the Copernican revolution. Not only are we not the center of the solar system or even of the galaxy, but also the Milky Way is merely a tiny island amidst a vast archipelago of countless galaxies. Many believe that

this suggests that mankind is just the result of a relatively minor cosmic accident and that life must have arisen countless times in the universe.

Others go so far as to conclude that the Copernican revolution has somehow disproved the Bible. Of course this erroneously supposes that the Bible claims that we are the center of the universe or at least in some preferred geographical location. While it is clear that mankind is the center of God's attention, that does not mean nor does the Bible claim that we are at some unique geographic position. The Bible does not address that issue.

In fact, this last step in the Copernican revolution should cause Christians to ponder the fact that despite our apparently insignificant location, the LORD has seen fit to concern himself with us. The modern view of the universe also allows us to better appreciate the mighty power of the Creator. We now better appreciate more than ever before that the heavens do declare the glory of God.

1. What is cosmology? What is cosmogony?

2. What was one proof that the ancients used to show that the earth was spherical?

3. What did Eratosthenes do?

4. What is the geocentric model?

5. What was Copernicus's great contribution?

6. What was the Tychonic model?

7. What were two discoveries that Galileo made with his telescope that challenged the thinking of his day?

8. What was William Herschel's contribution to cosmology?

9. What was the island universe theory?

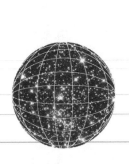

CHAPTER ONE

TWENTIETH-CENTURY COSMOLOGY

MODERN PHYSICS

For two centuries Newtonian physics had successes unparalleled in the history of science, but toward the end of the 19th century several experiments produced results that had not been anticipated. These results defied explanation with Newtonian physics, and this failure led in the early 20th century to what is called modern physics. Modern physics has two important pillars: quantum mechanics and general relativity. Quantum mechanics is the physics of small systems, such as atoms and subatomic particles. General relativity is the physics of very high speeds or of large concentrations of mass or energy. Both of these realms are beyond the scope of everyday experience, and so quantum mechanical and relativistic effects are not usually noticed. In other words, Newtonian mechanics, which is the physics of everyday experience, is a special case of modern physics.

Some creation scientists view both quantum mechanics and general relativity with suspicion. Part of the suspicion of quantum mechanics stems from the Copenhagen interpretation, a philosophical view of quantum mechanics. In quantum mechanics, the solution that describes location, velocity, and other properties of a particle is a wave function. The wave function amounts to a probability function. Where the value of the wave function is high, there is a high probability of finding the particle, and where the value of the wave function is low, there is a small probability of finding the particle. This result is pretty easy to understand when one considers a large number of particles — where the probability is high there is a greater likelihood of finding more particles.

However, how is one to interpret the result when considering only a single particle? The Copenhagen interpretation states that the particle exists in all possible states simultaneously. The particle exists in this weird state as long as no one observes the particle. Upon observation we say that the wave function collapses and the particle assumes some particular state. If the experiment is conducted often enough, the distribution of outcomes of the experiment matches the predictions of the probability function derived from the wave solution.

This suggests a fundamental uncertainty about the universe that runs counter to the Christian view of the world and an omniscient God. An omniscient God would presumably know the outcome of any experiment, an idea that is supported by the pre-determined world of Newtonian mechanics. With Newtonian mechanics if one knows all the properties, such as location and velocities of particles at one time, all such properties of the particles can be uniquely determined at any other time. This ability is called determinism. It would appear that quantum mechanics leads to a fundamental uncertainty that even God cannot probe. Uncertainty usually results from ignorance, that is, we lack enough input information to be able to calculate future states of a system. However, the uncertainty introduced by quantum mechanics is not one of ignorance, and so we call this uncertainty fundamental. By "fundamental uncertainty" we mean that even if we had infinite precision of all the relevant variables, we would still fail to predict the outcome of future experiments. Possible responses to this objection are that either the Copenhagen interpretation is wrong or that quantum mechanics is an incomplete theory. Phillip Dennis[1] has argued that quantum mechanics is probably an incomplete theory and that the uncertainty is no problem for the Christian.

One objection to modern relativity theory comes from the misappropriation of the term by moral relativists. Moral relativists claim that everything is relative and that general relativity has given physical evidence of this. General relativity says no such thing. In fact, it says just the opposite, that there are certain absolutes. Even if this assertion were true, this is a specious argument. Physical laws have no bearing upon morality and ethics. Another reservation about relativity that some creationists have is its perceived intimate relationship with the big-bang cosmogony. The reasoning seems to be that if the big bang is not true, then relativity is not true either. But the big bang is just one possible result from relativity. Creation-based cosmogonies could be generated with relativity theory, as has been attempted by Russ Humphreys.[2]

Those who doubt either or both pillars of modern physics also express discomfort with them, feeling that they just defy "common sense." However, there are many things about the world that defy common sense. For instance, the author of this book never ceases to be amazed by Newton's third law of motion, that when an object exerts a force upon another object, the second object exerts an opposite and equal force upon the first object. We shall see shortly that one of the questions addressed by general relativity is how gravitational force is transmitted through empty space. Newtonian physics simply hypothesizes that the force instantly and mysteriously acts over great distances. This too defies common sense. The important question for any theory is how well it describes reality.

Both theories of modern physics have been extensively tested in experiments and have proven to be very robust theories. These theories have been better established than almost any others in the history of science. Therefore in what follows it will be assumed that these models are correct, if not complete. Both theories play important roles in modern cosmology, but only relativity is significant in the historical development of modern cosmology, so further discussion of quantum mechanics will be deferred until the next chapter.

While many people worked on the foundation of modern relativity theory, Albert Einstein usually receives most credit. His special theory of relativity was published in 1905, followed by his general theory in 1916. The special theory is not that difficult to understand. It deals with the

situations of constant speeds near the speed of light. Suppose that a space ship were moving at 60% the speed of light toward a stationary person. Now suppose that the stationary person shined a light toward the moving astronaut. One might think that if the moving observer measured the speed of the light beam, that speed would be 160% the speed of light. If, on the other hand, the space ship were moving away, one might expect that the measured speed of the light would be 40% of the normal speed of light. However, actual measurement reveals that the speed of light is a constant no matter how much the observer may be moving. This sort of result was obtained by the famous Michelson-Morley experiment in 1887. This fact was one of the first experiments that showed the failure of classical Newtonian mechanics.

Einstein took the invariance of the speed of light as a postulate and examined the consequences. He found that near the speed of light, time must slow down as compared to time measured by someone who is not moving. The length of the spacecraft must decrease as speed increases, and the mass of the body must increase with increasing speed. These effects are respectively called time dilation, length contraction, and mass increase, and all have been confirmed in numerous experiments. Incidentally, special relativity predicts that mass increases toward infinity as speed approaches the speed of light. Thus, to achieve light speed would require an infinite amount of energy. This is impossible, so no particle that has mass can move as fast as the speed of light.

General relativity is concerned with accelerated motion at high speeds. Unfortunately it requires the use of complicated mathematical abstractions, and so it is not easy to understand. While we will not discuss any mathematical detail, we will

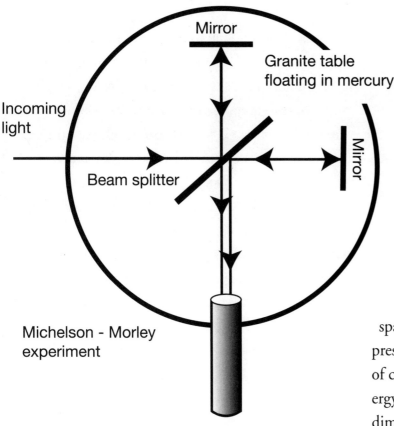

Mirror

Granite table
floating in mercury

Incoming
light

Mirror

Beam splitter

Michelson - Morley
experiment

Telescope

four dimensions of space. Any two dimensions of space could be represented as lines on graph paper, but instead of being flat like graph paper, the space is curved. The mathematics of curved space is similar to that of a curved sheet of graph paper.

What causes curvature of space? On a large scale it can be a property of space itself, but on the local level curvature results from the presence of matter or energy. It takes a large amount of energy or matter to curve space. Greater mass or energy will curve space by a greater amount. The mathematical expressions of general relativity describe the amount of curvature present as a result of the mass or energy. Keep in mind that space here refers to a four-dimensional manifold that includes time, so we should properly call it space-time. Objects move through space on straight paths called geodesics. If the space-time through which an object moves is flat, then that object will appear to us to move in a straight line or remain at rest. If on the other hand there is much matter or energy present so that the space-time is curved, the straight trajectory of the object through space-time will cause the object to appear to accelerate as we observe it.

While gravity is still a mysterious force, general relativity has removed some of the mystery and offered a more fundamental explanation than Newtonian theory. Newton posited that gravity reached great distances through empty space without any explanation, but general relativity offers a mechanism of how action at a distance works. The earth is following a geodesic in space-time. If the sun were not there, the space-time would not be curved and the earth would appear to us to move in a straight line. That is, the earth would not be accelerated. However, the large mass of the sun

qualitatively describe what the theory attempts to do.

As stated earlier, one question that general relativity attempts to explain is how gravitational force is transmitted through empty space. The sun is 93 million miles from the earth, and yet the earth somehow not only knows how far away the sun is, but also in which direction the sun is and how much mass the sun has. All of this information is necessary to determine the force of gravity. In Newtonian theory, gravitational force acts at a distance with no guess as to how the information necessary or the force is transmitted over the distance. General relativity answers this question by treating space as a real entity through which information can be transmitted like a wave. Space and time are handled in a similar fashion so that space can be thought of as consisting of four dimensions, three of space and one of time. The equations of general relativity tell how to treat the produces bending in space-time that is transmitted outward. At the location of the earth, the earth moves along a geodesic in the curved space-time. The earth's straight-line motion through curved space-time appears to us as acceleration.

Newtonian physics and general relativity treat space and time very differently. In Newtonian physics, space is not much more than a backdrop upon which masses move in time. Thus space, matter, and time are very distinct things. In general relativity, space and time are treated very similarly, and both have an intimate relationship with matter and energy. In Newtonian physics the presence of matter and energy have no effect upon space and time, while in general relativity they do. This is more than just a philosophical difference; it results in some definite differences in predictions that can be tested, as we shall now discuss.

At the time Einstein introduced his theory, people realized that an upcoming total solar eclipse offered an excellent opportunity to test general relativity. The theory predicts that as light passes near a large mass, the light rays should be slightly deflected toward the large mass due to the mass's gravity. Therefore if general relativity were true, stars observed near the edge of the sun during a total solar eclipse should appear a little closer to the sun than they would if general relativity were not true (see illustration on opposite page). During the 1919 total solar eclipse, a photograph was taken of the eclipsed sun and a number of stars near the edge of the sun. The positions of the stars were carefully measured and compared to their positions on a photograph made six months earlier. The shifts in the positions of the stars were consistent with the predictions of general relativity, and so this was hailed as the first confirmation of the theory.

There is a very small, but vocal minority of physicists who reject general relativity. They argue against this experiment on the basis that the errors in the measurements are very large and could have swamped the effect being measured. There is some legitimacy to this claim. The relativistic effect is very small and the errors of measurement and the corrections due to refraction of the earth's atmosphere were rather large. If this were the end of the matter, then the anti-relativists would have a basis of complaint here. But that was not the end of the matter. Similar experiments have been conducted during numerous eclipses since 1919, each with improving accuracy and agreement with the predictions of general relativity.

Furthermore, since the early 1970s, very long base interferometry (VLBI) has enabled us to repeat the experiment with much greater precision. VLBI combines simultaneous observations from widely separated radio telescopes to measure positions of radio sources with unprecedented accuracy. Distant point-radio sources that lie on the ecliptic (the plane of the earth's orbit around the sun) have had their positions in the sky measured with VLBI. Lying in the earth's orbital plane, the sun passes in front of these objects once each year. We can remeasure the positions of the point-radio sources when this happens. The differences in the measurements of the positions give us the amounts of shifts caused by the radio waves passing near the edge of the sun. The accuracy of the measured shifts in positions is orders of magnitude better than the accuracy of the 1919 eclipse shifts. This experiment has been repeated a number of times, and in every case the observed shifts match the predictions of general relativity very well.

When Einstein applied his field equations to the universe, his solution showed that his theory had difficulty explaining the universe as then understood. In the previous chapter we saw that Newton believed that the universe was eternal, but that his theory of gravity would cause the universe to have long ago collapsed upon itself. To avoid this difficulty Newton hypothesized that the universe was infinite in size. He reasoned that only then would all matter be attracted equally in all directions to produce a static universe. A static universe is one in which the matter is neither contracting nor expanding. But in Einstein's alternative theory of gravity even the appeal to an infinite universe failed. With general relativity, an infinite universe will eventually collapse upon itself, resulting in infinite density everywhere. This is obviously not the case, so Einstein had to solve this problem.

The answer that Einstein chose was to introduce what is called the cosmological constant into his solution. The cosmological constant, indicated by the Greek letter lambda (Λ), acts as a sort of anti-gravity. It amounts to a self-repulsion term that space has, but is locally very weak. However, over great distances this feeble space repulsion would accumulate to become an important factor in the structure of the universe. By finely tuning Λ to cancel the effect of gravity, Einstein was able to produce a static universe, as most people for some time thought that the universe must be. If Λ is not fine-tuned to counterbalance gravity, then the universe must either expand or contract.

The introduction of Λ was soon criticized, and Einstein later admitted that it was the biggest blunder that he ever made. However Einstein was much too harsh upon himself on this point. His field equations are differential equations, a type of calculus-based mathematics frequently encountered in the physical world. The general solution of a differential equation does contain a constant. Differential equations are frequently employed in physics, and the constants involved are usually set by the initial conditions of the problem. Often these constants turn out to be zero. The initial conditions of the universe determine what Λ is, but we do not know those initial conditions. Observations of the universe could tell us the value of Λ, but this is not an easy task. For decades most data have suggested that Λ is zero, but suggestions that it is nonzero continue to arise. If Λ is not fine-tuned to counterbalance gravity, then the universe must either expand or contract.

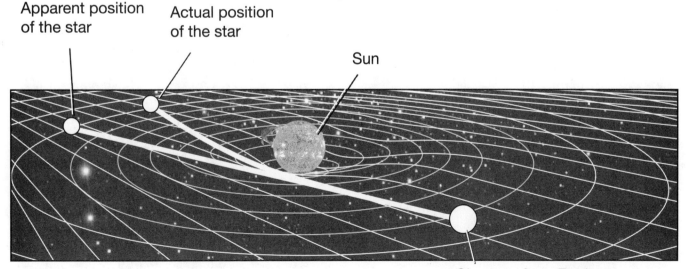

Apparent position of the star

Actual position of the star

Sun

Observer from Earth

THE EARLY BIG-BANG MODEL

Within two years of the publication of Einstein's theory of general relativity, a Belgian priest named Abbe LeMaitre had used it to produce the first model that presaged the currently accepted cosmological model, the big bang. LeMaitre called his model the "cosmic egg," which was rather simplistic by modern standards. He envisioned that the universe began with all of its matter and energy concentrated into a very hot sphere that expanded and cooled into the universe that we see today. One could ask how LeMaitre knew that the universe was expanding, rather than contracting or being static. One possibility is that he merely guessed, with some intuition from a definite and theistic origin of the universe in the finite past. That would have eliminated the static universe. It may have made more sense to him that the universe began small and expanded rather than starting large and then contracting, thus eliminating the contracting universe.

Another possibility is that LeMaitre may have known of the work of Vesto Slipher, a Lowell Observatory astronomer, just a few years earlier. In 1913 Slipher showed that many of the "nebulae" had large redshifts, indicative of speeds many hundreds or even thousands of kilometers per second away from us. This was a decade before the confirmation of the island universe theory, so these "nebulae" were not yet recognized as external galaxies. As members of our galaxy, the large redshifts of these "nebulae" made no sense, but if they were external galaxies, the redshifts made perfect sense in light of the predictions of Einstein's model: the universe is expanding.

After his confirmation of the island universe idea in 1924, Hubble certainly understood the significance of the redshifts of other galaxies. If this was evidence of the expansion of the universe, then there must also be a relationship between the amount of redshift and distance. Why are redshift and distance related? Anyone who has participated in or watched a 10-km race can see this. Within ten minutes of the start of the race, runners will be stretched out over considerable distance. The swiftest runners will be most distant from the starting line, while the slowest runners will be closest to the starting line. Runners of all intermediate speeds will be scattered between those extremes. As a result there will be a direct relationship between speed and distance from the starting line.

A similar thing will be true of galaxies. Those galaxies most distant now will be those that are made of material that was traveling away most swiftly at the beginning of the universe, while those that are closest now are made of material that was originally moving very slowly. It should be emphasized that this simple analogy, while useful for illustration, has several flaws. One is that the race involves only one spatial dimension while the expansion of the universe involves three. Another is that the analogy implies that the universe has a center and that the earth is near it. Most cosmological models today do not have a center. Lastly, the analogy implies that the measured redshifts are Doppler shifts due to motion through space. This is not true; Doppler shifts and redshifts are two very different things. This distinction and the lack of a center for the universe will be discussed in chapter 3.

In 1928 Hubble presented the relationship between the distance and redshift. This dependence has become known as the Hubble relation, and can be expressed as $Z = H_0 D$, where Z is the redshift, D is the distance, and H_0 is the constant of proportionality called the Hubble constant. Distances are usually expressed in mega parsecs (Mpc). An Mpc is a million parsecs, and a parsec is 3.26 light years, so an Mpc is 3.26 million light years. A light year is the distance that light travels in a year. Z can be expressed in km/sec, so the units of H_0 are km/sec Mpc. H_0 measures the expansion rate of the universe, and its value is the slope of the line representing the plot of redshift versus distance for a large number of galaxies. Measuring redshift by means of spectroscopy is straightforward and unambiguous, but finding distance is a difficult task and subject to many assumptions and potential errors. The appendix has a brief discussion of some of the methods of finding astronomical distances. Hubble initially found H_0 to be over 500 km/sec Mpc, but by the 1960s H_0 had been decreased to a little more than 50 km/sec Mpc. In the 1990s several studies suggested that H_0

be increased to about 80 km/sec Mpc. This is of more than academic interest, because it affects the age of the big-bang universe, which will be discussed later.

THE COSMOLOGICAL PRINCIPLE

Before the equations of general relativity are applied to the universe, a couple of assumptions are usually made. One assumption is that the universe is homogeneous. Homogeneity means that the universe has the same properties throughout. Of course homogeneity must include the universality of physical laws, or else science would not even be possible. In cosmology, homogeneity usually refers to the appearance and structure of the universe as well as the matter distribution. If the matter in the universe is clumpy, then the equations of general relativity cannot be applied easily, so this assumption is primarily based upon our ability to do the math. On a local level the universe appears very clumpy. For instance, in stars and planets the matter density is high, but in the vast expanses of space between stars and planets matter is almost non-existent.

This is a common problem in physics — we frequently encounter situations where the mass involved is clumpy. Consider a gas. We know that it is made of many tiny particles called atoms that are separated by distances that are large compared to the sizes of the atoms. However, from a macroscopic approach we can treat the gas as if it is made of some continuous fluid. At a macroscopic level the gas appears homogeneous and its clumpy microscopic nature can be ignored. Similarly, it is assumed that at some grand scale the universe is homogeneous, but at the largest scale so far probed (clusters of clusters of galaxies) the universe still appears clumpy. If the universe is in fact inhomogeneous, it is not known what effect that will have on our cosmology.

Another common assumption is that the universe is isotropic. Isotropy means that the universe has the same appearance or properties in all directions. This insures that the expansion is the same in all directions. If there were a net flow in one direction, then the universe would not be isotropic. There are other ways that the universe might not be isotropic. A few years ago some astronomers found that distant radio sources had their polarizations altered by amounts that depended upon distance but also upon direction in the sky. Polarization is a term used to describe the direction that waves are vibrating. A wave can vibrate in any direction perpendicular to the direction that the wave is traveling. Usually, electromagnetic waves vibrate in many directions, but frequently the waves oscillate predominantly in one direction. When this happens, we say that the wave is polarized. The observation that distant radio sources were polarized depending on their directions in space suggested that the universe is fundamentally different in different directions, that is, it is not isotropic.

The assumption of homogeneity and isotropy together is called the cosmological principle. The cosmological principle along with the observation of the expansion of the universe usually leads to the big-bang model. However the big-bang model is not the only possible model in an expanding universe governed by general relativity. The big-bang model forces one to accept that the universe had a beginning.

However, this possibility is unpalatable to many, as discussed previously, and also as witnessed by Einstein's fudging of the value of Λ to get a static, eternal universe.

Another attempt to produce an eternal universe starts with the assumption of the perfect cosmological principle. The perfect cosmological principle states that the universe has been homogeneous and isotropic at all times. The phrase "at all times" means that the universe always has and always will be as it is today. In this view, stars and galaxies are continually being born, growing old, and dying, but the universe remains the same forever. Since in this model the universe never changes, this is called the steady-state theory. You may ask, "if the universe is expanding, its average density should be decreasing, so how could the universe remain unchanged as per the steady-state theory?" In order for the steady-state universe to maintain a constant density, matter must spontaneously come into existence. Another name for the steady-state theory is the continuous creation theory. Some may object that this violates the law of conservation of matter, but the law of conservation of matter is merely a statement of how we see the universe operate. The rate of new matter production per unit volume required to maintain a constant density in the universe is so small as to escape our notice. Those who support the steady-state theory argue that the law of conservation of matter is only an approximation of how the universe really works.

In the 20 years prior to 1965 the steady-state theory enjoyed much support. Its appeal stemmed from the avoidance of a beginning and its ultimate simplicity and beauty. It was once described as being so beautiful that it must be true. Meanwhile the details of the competing model, the big bang, were being developed. One of the strongest supporters of the steady-state model, the late Sir Fred Hoyle, is credited with naming the other model when he, in exasperation, declared, "The universe did not begin in some big bang!" To Hoyle's chagrin, the name stuck, despite attempts to find a better name for it.

ALLEGED EVIDENCES OF THE BIG BANG

Several evidences against the steady-state theory have been presented, but the most devastating one was the 1964 (published in 1965) discovery of the 3K cosmic background radiation (CBR) by Arno Penzias and Robert Wilson. In 1978 Penzias and Wilson received the Nobel Prize in physics for their work. As researchers at the Bell labs in New Jersey, they were developing technology for microwave transmissions for communication. Penzias and Wilson had detected a background noise for which they could not find a source, and seemed to coming from all directions. In 1948 George Gamow had predicted that such a radiation should be seen throughout the universe, but the technology for detection did not exist at that time. By the 1960s the technology did exist, and Robert Dicke of Princeton University was planning the construction of equipment to observe the CBR when he happened to discuss the matter with Robert Wilson. Dicke encouraged Penzias and Wilson to publish their findings, along with a companion paper by Dicke that explained the significance of the find.

According to the big-bang model, the photons in the CBR came from a time when the universe was a few hundred thousand years old and at a temperature of about 3,000K. At that time most of the matter in the universe would have been protons and electrons, but the temperature and density were too high for hydrogen atoms to form. In this hot gas, photons would have been continually absorbed and reemitted so that the matter and energy would be in equilibrium and the radiation would have had a blackbody spectrum that was a function of the temperature at that time. As the universe expanded, the gas cooled and the density decreased to the point that stable hydrogen began to form and remained un-ionized as atoms. This time in the history of the universe is called the age of recombination, though a better name might be the age of combination, since the atoms did not previously exist.

According to the model, after the age of recombination, the matter in the universe no longer absorbed and reemitted all of the radiation, and the universe became transparent for the first time. Prior to the age of recombination, matter and energy were coupled in that the radiation could not escape the matter. Because light was so easily absorbed and reemitted, the mean free path of photons was extremely short. After the age of recombination the photon mean free path became virtually the size of the universe and energy managed to escape matter for the first time. We say that matter and energy would have become decoupled. The photons liberated during the age of recombination have traveled with little interaction in the ensuing 10-15 billion years. The photons have maintained a blackbody spectrum, but the universe has expanded a thousandfold in size since the age of recombination, so the blackbody spectrum has been redshifted by a factor of 1,000. The redshift reduced the effective temperature of the blackbody from 3,000K to 3K.

The steady-state theory does not predict the CBR, because in the steady-state theory the universe has always appeared the same as it does today, so there was never a time when the universe had a temperature of 3,000K. Some have hailed the CBR as one of the greatest discoveries of 20th century astronomy, because it eliminated the steady-state theory and "proved" the big-bang theory. Since the mid 1960s the big-bang model has reigned as the only viable model in the estimation of most cosmologists, so it has been dubbed the "standard cosmology." This does not mean that all opponents of the standard cosmology have given up. For years Hoyle continued to modify the steady-state theory so that it too would predict the CBR, but he was not successful. Hoyle and some of his associates, such as Geoff Burbidge and Halton Arp, have pointed out numerous problems with the big-bang theory. Some of these difficulties will be discussed in chapter 4.

The standard cosmology has been a very robust and quantitative model, as indicated by the many highly technical papers on the subject published each year. When asked how astronomers know that the big bang is the correct scenario of the origin of the universe, three evidences are usually put forth. One evidence is the CBR, as just discussed. The other two are the expansion of the universe and the abundances of the light elements. But how good are these evidences? Before answering this question, we should investigate just a bit the nature of proof and prediction in science.

PROOF AND PREDICTION

A scientific theory is judged upon how well it explains data. Data may be divided into classes: the data already in hand when the theory is developed and new data from experiments inspired by the theory. The data already available are used to guide the construction of a theory. A good theory should be able to account for all, or at least most, of that data. In other words, a theory should be able to explain what we already know. If it does, then we say that the theory has good explanatory power. If a theory does not have good explanatory power, then it should be modified so that it does or should be replaced by another theory that does.

Once a theory is developed, it can be used to make certain predictions about the results of experiments. When an experiment is performed, the predictions of the theory can be compared to the data from the experiment. If the predictions match the data, then we say that the theory has been "proved," though proof in this context is a bit different from what is meant in deductive reasoning or even in everyday use. A better choice of words would be to say that the theory is confirmed. If the theory's predictions do not match the data, then the theory has been disproved, and the theory must be either modified or replaced. One strange aspect of science is that while we can disprove theories, being totally certain that any theory is absolutely correct is not possible. The history of science is filled with theories that once enjoyed proof or confirmation only to ultimately be disproved. Examples of these discarded theories include the phlogiston theory of combustion, the caloric theory of heat, and abiogenesis.

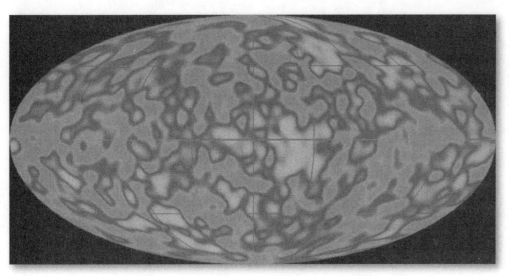

Cosmic background radiation (CBR) image

We can say that a theory has predictive power if its predictions have been tested by experimentation. Many theories have explanatory power but lack predictive power. This is especially true of the historical sciences. Much of the alleged proof for biological evolution is explanatory rather than predictive in nature. Evolution is purported to explain what we observe, but it is difficult to conceive of experiments that could clearly test what has happened in the past. The same is true of creation. In either case the question of falsifiability arises. If no experiment can be conducted that could possibly disprove the theory, then the theory is not falsifiable. Any number of scenarios could be concocted to explain a phenomenon, but the mere explanation of the facts in hand hardly constitutes proof. A good theory should possess both explanatory power and predictive power.

Are the three evidences for the big bang explanatory or predictive in nature? The expansion of the universe is definitely explanatory and not predictive. General relativity suggested that the universe should be expanding or contracting, but it could not predict which. The fact that the universe is expanding could only be determined observationally. Much later the big-bang model was developed to explain the datum that the universe is expanding. Any number of models could be constructed to explain the expansion. The steady-state model was one of those attempts. Neither cosmology predicted the expansion, but they merely responded to that fact as a means of explanation.

The evidence concerning the abundances of the light elements is subtler, but this too appears to be explanatory rather than predictive. The elements in question here are hydrogen, deuterium, a rare heavier isotope of hydrogen, the two isotopes of helium (He_3 and He_4) and lithium. Each of these elements would have been produced in the first few minutes of the big bang. All the heavier elements are presumed to have formed in stars. The big-bang cosmology does predict the abundances of the light elements, but most people fail to realize that information concerning elemental abundances was input in creating the model. Knowledge of the light element abundances was required in constraining which subset of possible models was viable. In fact, small changes in our understanding of these abundances have allowed cosmologists to fine-tune their models. It would be most strange if a model did not "predict" the parameters that were input for the theory. It would show that the model was internally inconsistent.

The CBR does appear to be a clean prediction of the big-bang model. The CBR was first predicted nearly two decades before its discovery. Even though the discovery by Penzias and Wilson was serendipitous, there were others who were making plans to mount a search for the CBR. The big-bang model could not predict the exact temperature of the CBR, but an estimate of the range of temperature was possible. The measured temperature was near the lower end of the range. The CBR is real, and its existence has been confirmed many times. Therefore denying its existence is not an option. The extremely smooth shape of the CBR spectrum is difficult to explain any other way. The CBR elevates the status of the predictive power of the standard cosmology. It is the only prediction of the theory. Further studies of the CBR will be discussed in the next chapter.

THE GEOMETRY OF THE UNIVERSE

Before moving onto other topics, a few concepts about the geometry of the universe should be addressed. Space can be bound or unbound. Being bound refers to space having an edge or boundary. In two-dimensional space, a tabletop is bound, because it has a definite boundary, the edge of the tabletop. On the other hand, a mathematical plane would be unbound, because it extends indefinitely in all directions and hence has no boundary. It is difficult to conceive of our three spatial dimensions being bound. If space had a boundary, one must wonder what the nature of the boundary would be. Would it be some sort of wall that would forbid us to cross? If so, of what would the wall be made, and why could we not cross it? Would there be another side, and if so, what would it be like and could information pass through the wall? If these sorts of questions had any real answers, then it would seem that the other side of the boundary is part of our universe as well, so the wall is not really an edge after all. On the other hand, a universe without a boundary would seem to extend forever and would thus be infinite in size. As difficult a concept that a bound universe may be, a universe that has no spatial end is scarcely easier for the human mind to comprehend.

So we seem to be stuck with the choice between an infinite and unbound universe and a universe that is finite and bound. Is there a way past this dilemma? Yes. Recall that according to general relativity space may have some overall curvature. It is possible that space may curve back upon itself so that it has no boundary, but it is finite in size. Consider a two dimensional example. A flat, two-dimensional object, such as a piece of paper, is usually finite in size and has a boundary. On the other hand, the surface of the earth is two-dimensional, but it is curved back onto itself. Therefore, the surface of the earth has no boundary or edge, but it is finite in size. If you traveled in a straight line on the earth's surface you would eventually return to your starting point. In like fashion, if the universe is closed back on itself and if you traveled in a straight line, you would eventually return to your starting point. Such a universe would be finite in size and unbound, and thus we could avoid both an infinite universe and a bound universe.

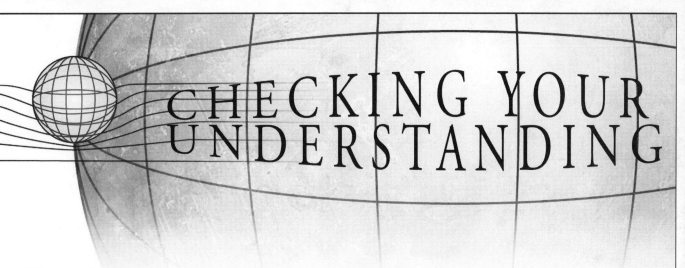

CHECKING YOUR UNDERSTANDING

1. What are the two pillars of modern physics?

2. What is the main difference between the Newtonian physics and the modern physics views of gravity?

3. What was the first confirmation of Einstein's theory of general relativity?

4. What is a static universe?

5. What is the cosmological constant?

6. What does homogeneity mean?

7. What does isotropy mean?

8. What is the cosmological principle? What model usually stems from the assumption of the cosmological principle?

9. What is the perfect cosmological principle? What model usually follows from the assumption of the perfect cosmological principle?

10. What is the significance of the cosmic background radiation?

11. Why are the expansion of the universe and the abundances of the light elements not proper evidence for the big-bang theory?

12. What does it mean for the universe to be bound?

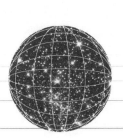

CHAPTER TWO

MORE RECENT DEVELOPMENTS IN COSMOLOGY

Until the 1960s, many people did not take cosmology seriously. While the musings of cosmologists were fascinating, they remained just that for lack of definitive data. The situation began to change with the discovery of the CBR in 1964. In the wake of that discovery, additional relevant data began to be found, and many new theories were developed. One of the more peculiar ideas was the realization that particle physics had much to tell us about cosmology. The peculiarity comes from considering the intimate relationship between the study of the smallest things (particle physics) and the largest thing (cosmology). Since the 1970s many exciting things have been happening in cosmology.

What follows in this chapter is a discussion of various cosmological ideas, in which it may often appear as if the author agrees with these ideas or with the big-bang theory. We should emphasize that this is only for the sake of discussion. In a later chapter we will see how the big-bang cosmology and related ideas discussed here are in conflict with the creation account in the book of Genesis. To discuss these concepts for now it is easiest to treat them as if they are acceptable, setting aside for a time the question of whether they are consistent with a biblical world view. In other words, we ask that you put on a "big-bang hat" to engage in this discussion. Please do not take from the discussion in this chapter that the author supports the big-bang model or that he has any enthusiasm for it.

THE RATE OF EXPANSION AND THE FLATNESS PROBLEM

As the universe expands, the rate of expansion is slowed by the gravity of matter in the universe. An analogy can be made to an object that is projected upward from the surface of the earth. The speed of the object will slow due to the earth's gravity. For small speeds the object will quickly reverse direction and fall back to the earth. As the initial speed is increased, the object will move to higher altitudes before falling back to earth. There is a minimum speed, called the escape velocity, for which the object will not return to the earth's surface. At the earth's surface the escape velocity is about 25,000 mph. Theoretically, an object moving at escape velocity will eventually arrive at an infinite distance from the earth with

no remaining speed. Objects moving faster than the escape velocity will never return, but they will never come to rest. Space probes to the moon or other planets must be accelerated above the escape velocity. The more that their speeds exceed the escape velocity, the shorter time their trips will take.

The universe should behave in a similar way. If the expansion is too slow, gravity will eventually reverse the direction so that the universe will contract once again. This presumably would lead to a sort of reverse of the big bang that is usually called the "big crunch." This would also result in a finite lifetime for the universe. If the expansion exceeds some value akin to the escape velocity, the expansion will be slowed, but not enough to reverse the expansion. In this scenario the universe will expand forever, and as it does its density will continually decrease.

The escape velocity of the earth depends upon its mass and size. In a similar fashion, the

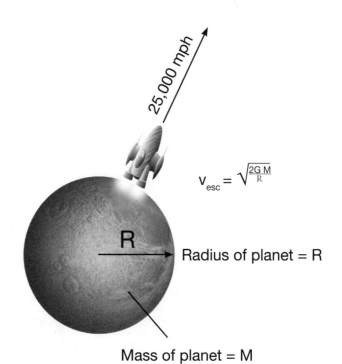

$$v_{esc} = \sqrt{\frac{2GM}{R}}$$

Radius of planet = R

Mass of planet = M

Escape velocity of a spaceship

question of whether our universe will expand forever or contract back upon itself depends upon the size and mass of the universe. An easier way to express this is in terms of one variable (rather than two) such as the density, which depends upon both mass and size. There exists a critical density above which the universe will expand forever and below which it will halt expansion and collapse upon itself. If the universe possesses the critical density, its expansion will asymptotically approach zero and never collapse.

One of the parameters used to describe the universe is Ω (the Greek letter omega), defined to be the ratio of the total gravitational potential energy to the total kinetic energy. Gravitational potential energy is energy that an object possesses because of its mass and any gravity present. On the earth, some object with elevation has gravitational potential energy. Examples would include a car parked on a hill or water behind a dam. The higher the hill or the higher the dam, the more energy there is. The more powerful hydroelectric dams are those that are higher and have larger amounts of water behind them. As the water is allowed to fall from its original height and pass through a turbine, the gravitational potential energy is converted to electrical energy. Kinetic energy is energy of motion. A speeding bullet contains far more energy than a slowly moving bullet.

Since the universe has mass and hence gravity, it must have gravitational potential energy as well. The expansion of the universe represents motion, so the universe must have kinetic energy as well. As the universe expands, the gravitational potential energy will change. At the same time, gravity will slow the rate of expansion so that the amount of kinetic energy will change as well.

Generally the two energies will not change in the same sense or by the same amount so that Ω will change with time. A value of $\Omega < 1$ means that the kinetic energy is greater than the gravitational potential energy. Conversely, a value of $\Omega > 1$ means that the gravitational potential energy exceeds the kinetic energy. If a big-bang universe began with $\Omega < 1$, then Ω will decrease in value. The minimum value is zero. If on the other hand $\Omega > 1$ at the beginning of the universe, then Ω should have increased in value. Therefore, over billions of years the value of Ω should have dramatically changed from its initial value. For several decades all data have suggested that while Ω is indeed less than 1, it is not much less than 1. The sum of all visible matter in the universe produces an Ω equal to about 0.1. The prospect of dark matter pushes the value of Ω closer to 1.

The fact that Ω is very close to 1 today suggests that the universe began with Ω almost, if not exactly, equal to 1. If Ω were only a few percent less than 1 initially, then the evolution of the universe since the big bang should have produced an Ω dramatically less (many orders of magnitude) than 1 today. How close to 1 did the value of Ω have to be at the beginning of the universe to produce the universe that we see today? The value depends upon certain assumptions and the version of the big bang that one uses, but most estimates place the initial value of Ω equal to 1 to within 15 significant figures. That is, the original value of Ω could not have deviated from 1 any more than the 15th place to the right of the decimal point. Why should the universe have Ω so close to 1? This problem is called the flatness problem. The name comes from the geometry of a universe where Ω is exactly equal to 1. In such a universe space would have no curvature and hence would be flat. There are several possible solutions to the flatness problem.

One possible answer to the flatness problem is that this is just how the world happens to be. While this is not a physical impossibility, it does raise some troubling questions, at least for the atheist. It seems that the initial value of Ω could have been any number, but only a very small range in values could have led to a universe in which we exist. If Ω were too small, then the universe would have rapidly expanded to the point that the density would have been too low for stars and galaxies to form. Thus there could have been no planets and no life. Ergo, we would not have evolved to observe the universe. If on the other hand the value of Ω were initially too large, the universe would have ceased expanding long ago and contracted back to a "big crunch."

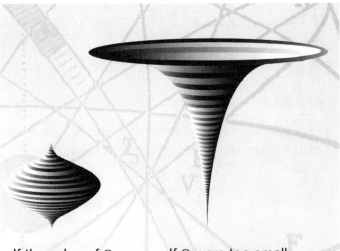

If the value of Ω were too large the universe would have ceased expanding long ago and collapsed in on itself.

If Ω were too small, then the universe would have rapidly expanded to the point that the density would have been too low for stars and galaxies to form.

This would not have allowed enough time for us to evolve. Either way, we should not exist. Therefore the correct conditions that would have allowed our existence were present in the universe from the beginning.

THE ANTHROPIC PRINCIPLE

Nor is the value of Ω the only feature of the universe fit for our existence. Scientists have identified a number of other parameters upon which our existence depends. Examples include the masses and charges of elementary particles, as well as the constants, such as the permittivity of free space, that govern their interactions. If some of these constants had slightly different values, then stable atoms as we know them would not be possible or the unique properties of carbon and water upon which life depends would not exist. All of these quantities are fundamental, that is, they do not depend upon other parameters, but are instead numbers that had to assume some values. There is no reason why those constants have the values that they have, other than the fact that they just do. Of all the random permutations of the constants that could have occurred, our universe exists as it does with these particular numbers. What is the probability that the universe would assume parameters that would be conducive to life, or even demand that life exist? To some it appears that the universe is designed; from its beginning the universe was suitable for our existence. In the early 1970s a scientist named Brandon Carter dubbed this line of reasoning the anthropic principle.[1]

To many Christians this constitutes strong evidence of God's existence and has become part of their apologetics.[2] Of course, use of the anthropic principle assumes that the big-bang cosmogony is correct. There is much difficulty in reconciling the big bang to a faithful rendering of the Genesis creation account, a topic that will be explored in a later chapter.

To atheists and agnostics the case is not nearly as clear. How do they resolve this issue? They try several approaches. One is to argue that the probability question has been improperly formulated. They maintain that one should ask what the probability of the existence of something is only before that something is actually observed. Once the object in question is known to exist, its probability that it exists with specified characteristics is 1, no matter how unlikely it may seem to us.

I can use myself as an example. If one considers the genetic makeup of my parents, it is obvious that there were literally billions of different combinations of children that my parents could have had. Each potential child would have had unique features, such as sex, height, build, and eye and hair color, to mention just a few. My parents only had two children, so it would seem that I am extremely improbable. Yet, when people meet me for the first time, they are not (usually!) amazed by my existence. Most people recognize that given that I exist, I must exist in some state. Therefore the probability that I exist as I do is 1. They argue that the incredible odds against my having the traits that I have only make sense if the probability were asked before I was conceived. In like fashion the universe exists, so the probability that it exists as it does must be 1. Therefore, they claim, we should not be shocked that the universe exists as it does.

How does one respond to this answer? We shall see in chapter 4 that a similar argument is used against the work of the astronomer Halton Arp, so the discussion there would apply here as well. We will repeat some of that here. We use probability arguments all of the time to eliminate improbable explanations. DNA testing is now used in many criminal cases. If there is a tissue sample

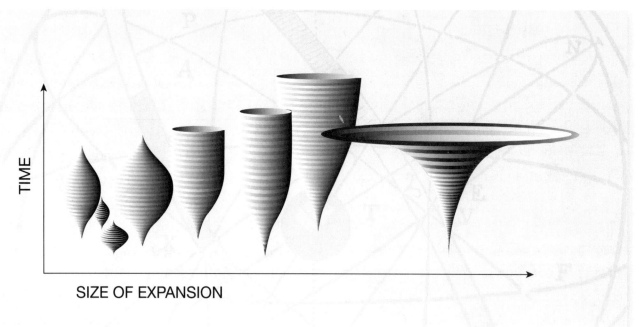

TIME

SIZE OF EXPANSION

On the left of the illustration are those universes that collapsed back on themselves before life could begin and on the right are those universes that expanded too quickly and will continue to expand forever.

of the perpetrator of a crime left at the scene of the crime, then DNA often can be extracted. The sample may be skin or blood cells, hair, or even saliva on a cigarette butt. Comparison of the DNA from the sample with DNA extracted from a suspect can reveal how well the two DNA samples match. Often this is expressed as how improbable it would be for two people selected at random to share the same DNA. If the probability were as little as one in a million, then that would be considered solid evidence of guilt to most people. However, a defense attorney may argue that as unlikely as a match between his innocent client and the truly guilty party is, the match actually happened so the probability is 1. That argument alone without any other evidence to exonerate the defendant is obviously very lame and would not convince any competent juror. Yet, this answer to Arp's work asks us to believe a similar argument.

There are other possible answers to the anthropic principle. For instance, some cosmologists suggest that our universe may not be unique.[3] Our universe may be just one of many or even infinite universes. This concept of a "multi-verse" will be discussed further shortly. In this view each separate universe has its own unique properties, a few having properties that allow for life, but most being sterile. We could not exist in most of the universes, so it should not surprise us that we exist in a universe that is conducive for life. This explanation gets very close to the essence of the response to the anthropic principle discussed above. The only difference is that this answer seeks to explain our existence by appealing to a large sample size. The reader should note that this sort of answer is hardly scientific (how could it be tested?), and amounts to rather poor philosophy at best.

INFLATION

Returning to the flatness problem, a radically different answer was pursued in the early 1980s. Late in 1979 Alan Guth suggested that the early universe might have undergone an early rapid expansion. According to this scenario, shortly after the big bang (somewhere between 10^{-37} and 10^{-34} seconds after the big bang) when the universe was still very small, the universe quickly expanded in size by many orders of magnitude (the increase in the size of the universe might have been from the size of an elementary particle to about the size of a grapefruit). This behavior has been called inflation. Inflation would have happened far faster than the speed of light. To some people this appears to be a violation of Einstein's theory of special relativity, which tells us that material objects cannot move as fast as the speed of light, let alone faster than light. However, in the inflationary model objects do not move faster than the speed of light, but rather space expands faster than light and carries objects along with it. The initial value of Ω may have not been particularly close to 1, but as a result of inflation it was driven to be almost identically equal to 1. Therefore the universe was not fine-tuned from the beginning, but rather was forced to be flat through a very natural process. Inflation solves the flatness problem without invoking the anthropic principle as another potential difficulty.

Inflation can explain several difficulties other than the flatness problem. One of these is the homogeneity of the universe. The CBR appears to have the same temperature in every direction. If two objects that have different temperatures are brought together so that they may exchange heat, we say that they are in thermal contact. Once

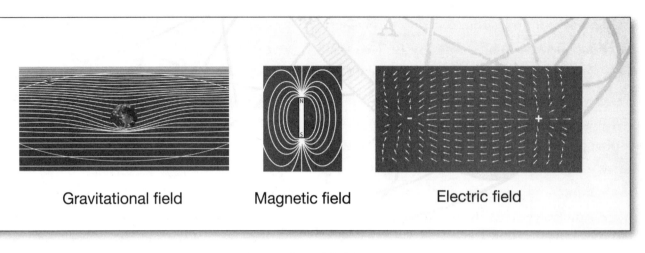

Examples of fields

the two objects no longer exchange heat while still in thermal contact, they must have the same temperature and we say that they have come into thermal equilibrium. Regions of the universe that are diametrically opposite from our position and from which we are now receiving the CBR have yet to come into thermal contact, yet those regions have the same temperature. How can that be if they have not been in thermal contact before? This problem is often called the horizon problem, because parts of the universe that should not have come into contact yet would be beyond each other's horizon. In an inflationary universe, very small regions of the universe could have come into thermal equilibrium before inflation happened. After inflation, the regions could have been removed from thermal contact until thermal contact was reestablished much later. With this possibility, widely dispersed regions had been in thermal equilibrium earlier, so it is not surprising that they are still in thermal equilibrium.

What mechanism drives inflation? Two classes of solutions have been suggested. One possibility is an energy field, called an "inflaton," that fills the universe. Fields are used in physics to describe a number of phenomena. Examples of

fields are gravitational fields that surround masses, electric fields around charges, and magnetic fields around magnets. Fields can be thought of as permeating and altering space. The release of the inflaton's energy would have powered inflation.

An alternate suggestion is that inflation was powered by a process that is sometimes called "symmetry breaking." There are four recognized fundamental forces of nature: gravitational force, the electromagnetic force, and the weak and 9s. All observed forces could be described as manifestations of one of these fundamental forces. The history of physics is one of gradual unification of various, apparently disparate, forces. For instance, during the early and middle parts of the 19th century, a series of experimental results suggested that electrical and magnetic phenomena were related. A set of four equations formulated by James Clerk Maxwell unified electricity and magnetism into a single theory of electromagnetism. During the 1970s a theory that united electromagnetic forces with the weak nuclear force was established. In fact, Steven Weinberg, whose very famous popular-level book on the big bang, *The First Three Minutes*, shared the 1978 Nobel Prize in physics for his contribution in this unification. While the electromagnetic and weak nuclear forces have different manifestations today, the unification of these two forces into a single theory means that they would have been a single phenomenon at the much higher temperatures present in an early big-bang universe. With this unification we can say that there are now three fundamental forces of nature.

Most physicists believe that all the forces of nature can be combined into a single theory. Work is progressing on a theory that will unify all of the fundamental forces, save gravity. Gravity is believed to be hard to unify with the others, because gravity is so much weaker than the other forces. If and when such a theory is found, it will be called a grand unified theory (GUT). Physicists hope that one day gravity can be combined with a GUT to produce a theory of everything (TOE). Much research is dedicated to finding a GUT, and there are several different approaches to the search. Almost all involved agree that the unification of forces would only happen at very high energies and temperatures. This is why attempts at developing a GUT require the use of huge particle accelerators — bigger accelerators produce higher energies. Cosmologists think that the temperature of the very early universe would have been high enough for all of the forces of nature to be unified. This unity of forces represents a sort of symmetry. As the universe expanded and cooled, the forces would have separated out one by one. Being the weakest by far, gravity would have separated first and then been followed by the others. Each separation would have been a departure from the initially simpler state, introducing a form of asymmetry in the forces of nature. Therefore the separation of each force from the single initial force is called symmetry breaking.

Symmetry breaking is similar to a phase transition in matter. When ice melts, it requires the absorption of energy that cools the environment of the ice. Likewise when water freezes it releases energy into the environment. When symmetry breaking occurs, energy is released into the universe. This energy powers the inflation. Many cosmologists think that it is possible that the universe could undergo another symmetry-breaking episode with potentially cataclysmic results for humanity. Of course, without any knowledge of the relevant physics required, it is impossible to predict when or even if such a thing is likely.

Since its inception there have been thousands of papers written about the inflationary universe, and there have been more than 50 variations of inflationary theories proposed. Because inflation has been able to explain several difficult problems, it will probably remain a major player in big-bang cosmology for some time to come. Almost no one has noticed that there are no direct observational tests for inflation, its appeal being directly a result of its ability to solve some cosmological problems. The inflation model plays an important role in origin scenarios of the big bang, as we shall see shortly.

STRING THEORY

Another new idea important in cosmology is string theory. String theory posits that all matter consists of very small entities that behave like tiny vibrating strings. In addition to the familiar three dimensions of space, string theory requires that there be at least six more spatial dimensions. This brings the total number of dimensions to ten, nine spatial and one time dimension. Why have we not noticed these extra dimensions? Since the early universe, these dimensions have been "rolled up" into an incredibly small size so that we cannot see them. Nevertheless, these dimensions would have played an important role in the behavior of matter and the universe early in its history. This introduces the relationship between cosmology and particle physics. The unification of physical laws presumably existed in the high energy of the early universe. Since the interactions of fundamental particles would have been very strong in the early universe, the proper theory of those interactions must be included in cosmological models.

Many popular-level books have been written on string theory. Even the Christian astronomer (and progressive creationist) Hugh Ross has weighed in with a treatise[4] where he invokes string theory to explain a number of theological questions. What is easy to miss in all of these writings is that string theory is a highly speculative theory for which there is yet no evidence. It may be some time before this situation changes. Among cosmologists the tentative nature of string theory is recognized, and there are other possible theories of elementary particles.

DARK MATTER

Galaxies tend to be found in groups called clusters. Large clusters of galaxies may contain over a thousand members. Astronomers assume that these clusters are gravitationally bound; that is, that the members of a cluster follow stable orbits about a common center of mass. In the 1930s the astronomer Fritz Zwicky measured the speeds of galaxies in a few clusters. He found that the individual galaxies were moving far too fast to be gravitationally bound, a fact since confirmed for many other clusters. This means that the member galaxies are flying apart and over time the clusters will cease to exist. The break-up time of a typical cluster is on the order of a billion years or so, far less than the presumed age of the clusters. Some creationists cite this as evidence that the universe may be far younger than generally thought. In other words, the upper limit to the age of these structures imposed by dynamical considerations might be evidence left by our Creator.

To preserve the antiquity of clusters of galaxies, astronomers have proposed that the clusters

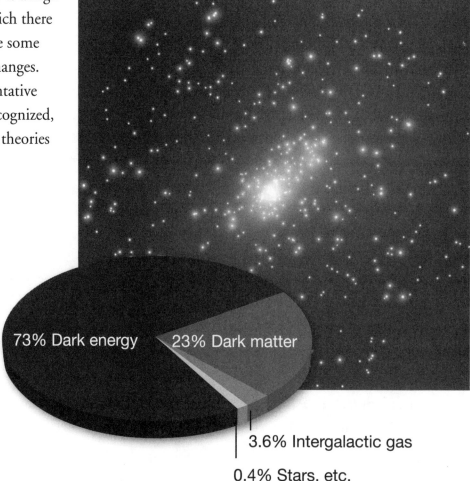

73% Dark energy   23% Dark matter

3.6% Intergalactic gas

0.4% Stars, etc.

contain much more matter than we think. There are two ways to measure the mass of a cluster of galaxies. One is to measure how much light the galaxies in the cluster give off (luminous mass). Counting the number of galaxies involved and measuring their brightnesses give us an estimate of the mass of a cluster. Studies of the masses and total light of stars in the solar neighborhood give us an idea of how much mass corresponds to a given amount of light. The second way to estimate the mass is to calculate how much mass is required to gravitationally bind the members of the cluster given the motions of those members (dynamic mass). Comparison of these two methods shows that in nearly every case the dynamic mass is far larger than the luminous mass. In some cases the luminous mass is less than 10% of the dynamic mass.

If the dynamic mass calculations are the true measure of the masses of clusters of galaxies, then this suggests that the vast majority of mass in the universe is unseen. This has been dubbed dark matter. If this were the only data supporting the existence of dark matter, then suspicion of the reality of dark matter would be quite warranted. However, in 1970 other evidence began to mount for the existence of dark matter. In that year an astronomer found that objects in the outer regions of the Andromeda Galaxy were orbiting faster than they ought. This was unexpected. Gravitational theory suggests that within the massive central portion of a galaxy, from which most of its light originates, the speeds of orbiting objects should increase linearly with a distance from the center. This is confirmed by observation. However, theory also suggests that farther out from the central portion of a galaxy (beyond where most of the mass appears to be) orbital speeds should be Keplerian. Orbiting bodies are said to follow Keplerian motion if they follow the three laws of planetary motion discovered by Kepler four centuries ago. An alternate statement of Kepler's third law is that orbital speeds are inversely proportional to the square root of the distance from the center. What was found instead is that the speeds of objects very far from the center are independent of distance or even increase slightly with distance. Similar behavior has been found in other galaxies, including the Milky Way.

This strange behavior for objects orbiting galaxies at great distances is independent evidence for dark matter, but it also tells where dark matter resides. If these objects are truly orbiting, then basic physics demands that much matter must exist within the orbits of these bodies, but beyond the inner galactic regions where most of the light comes. These outer regions are called the halos of galaxies. Since there is little light coming from galactic halos, this matter must be dark. Estimates of the amount of halo dark matter required to produce the observed orbits are consistent with the estimates from clusters of galaxies. Both suggest that, like an iceberg, what we see only accounts for about 10% of the mass.

What is the identity of dark matter? There have been many proposed theories. "Normal" matter consists of atoms made of protons, neutrons and electrons. The masses of the neutron and proton are very similar, but the mass of the electron is about a factor of 1,800 less massive than the proton or neutron. Protons and neutrons belong to a class of particles called baryons. Since most of the mass of atoms is accounted for by baryons, "normal" matter is said to be baryonic. We would be most comfortable with baryonic solutions to the dark matter question, but baryonic matter is difficult to make invisible. While faint stars are by far the most common type of stars and hence account for most stellar mass, low mass stars are so faint that the light of galaxies is dominated by brighter, more massive stars. However, even if dark matter consisted entirely of extremely faint stars, their combined light would be easily visible. If the matter were in much smaller particles such as dust, the infrared emission from the dust would be easily detected. Some have proposed that dark matter is contained in many planet-sized objects. This solution, dubbed MACHO (for MAssive Compact Halo Object), avoids the detectable emission of larger and smaller objects just mentioned. There has been an extensive search for MACHOs, and there is some data to support this identification though this is still controversial.

More exotic candidates for dark matter abound. Some suggest that dark matter consists of many black holes that do not interact with their surroundings enough to be detected with radiation. Another idea is that if neutrinos have mass, then large clouds of neutrinos in galactic halos might work. During the summer of 2001 strong evidence was found that neutrinos indeed have mass. Alternatively, heretofore-unknown particles have been proposed. One is called WIMPS, for Weakly Interacting Massive ParticleS. Obviously MACHO was named in direct competition with WIMPS. The identity of dark matter is another example of how cosmology and particle physics could be intimately related.

The relationship of dark matter to cosmology should be obvious. The fate of the universe is tied to the value of Ω, and Ω depends upon the amount of matter in the universe. If 90% of the matter in the universe is dark, then Ω could be very close to 1, and dark matter would have a profound effect upon the evolution of the universe over billions of years. The presence of dark matter would have been vitally important in the development of structure in the early universe. The universe is generally assumed to have been very smooth right after the big bang. This assumption is partly based upon simplicity of calculation, but also upon the unstable nature of inhomogeneities in mass. If the matter in the universe had appreciably clumped, then those clumps would have acted as gravitational seeds to attract additional matter and hence would have grown in mass. If those gravitational seeds were initially too great, then nearly all of the matter in the universe would have been sucked into massive black holes leaving little mass to form galaxies, stars, planets, and people. If, on the other hand, the mass in the early universe were too smooth, there would have been no effective gravitational seeds, and no structures such as galaxies, stars, planets, and people could have arisen. The range of homogeneity in which the initial conditions of the big bang existed and given rise to the universe that we now see must have been quite small. This is another example of the fine-tuning that the universe has apparently undergone that to some suggests the anthropic principle.

If dark matter exists, then its role in a big-bang universe must be assessed. Most considerations include how much dark matter exists and in what form. The dark matter may be hot or cold, depending upon how fast the matter was moving. If the dark matter moved quickly then it is termed hot. Otherwise it is cold. The speed depends upon the mass and identity of dark matter. It should be obvious that at this time dark matter is a rather free parameter in cosmology.

THE COBE AND WMAP EXPERIMENTS

The early universe must have had some slight inhomogeneity in order to produce the structure that we see today. If there were no gravitational seeds to collect matter, then we would not be here to observe the universe. Cosmologists have managed to calculate about how much inhomogeneity must have existed in the big bang. This inhomogeneity would have been present at the age of recombination when the radiation in the CBR was allegedly emitted. The CBR should be very uniform, but the inhomogeneity would have been imprinted upon the CBR as localized regions that are a little warmer or cooler than average. Predictions of how large the inhomge-

neities should be led to the design of the COBE (COsmic Background Explorer, pronounced KOB-EE) satellite. COBE was designed to accurately measure the CBR over the entire sky and measure the predicted fluctuations in temperature.

The two-year COBE experiment ended in the early 1990s with a perfectly smooth CBR. This means that temperature fluctuations predicted by models then current were not found. Eventually a group of researchers used a very sophisticated statistical analysis to find subtle temperature fluctuations in the smooth data. Variations of one part in 10^5 were claimed. Subsequent experiments that were more limited in scope were claimed to verify this result. These have been hailed as confirmation of the standard cosmology.

However, there are some lingering questions. For instance, while the COBE experiment was designed to measure temperature variations, the variations allegedly found were an order of magnitude less than those predicted. Yet this is hailed as a great confirmation of the big-bang model. Some have written

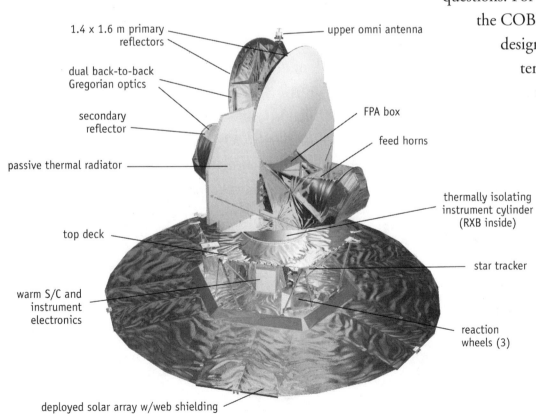

1.4 x 1.6 m primary reflectors

dual back-to-back Gregorian optics

secondary reflector

passive thermal radiator

top deck

warm S/C and instrument electronics

deployed solar array w/web shielding

upper omni antenna

FPA box

feed horns

thermally isolating instrument cylinder (RXB inside)

star tracker

reaction wheels (3)

WMAP (Wilkinson Microwave Anisotropy Probe)

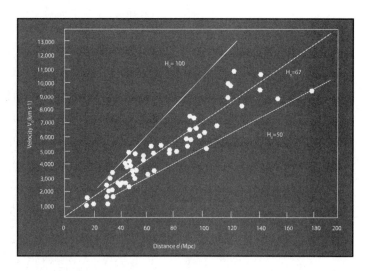

The Hubble constant describes how fast objects appear to be moving away from our galaxy as a function of distance. If you plot apparent recessional velocity against distance, as in the figure above, the Hubble constant is simply the slope of a straight line through the data.

that the COBE results perfectly matched predictions, but this is simply not true. Since the COBE results, some theorists have recalculated big-bang models to produce the COBE measurements, but this hardly constitutes a perfect match. Instead, the data have guided the theory rather than the theory predicting the data.

Another fact that has been lost by many people is that the alleged variations in temperature were below the sensitivity of the COBE detectors. How can an experiment measure something below the sensitivity of the device? The variations became discernable only after much processing of the COBE data with high-powered statistics. One of the COBE researchers admitted that he could not point to any direction in the sky where the team had clearly identified a hotter or cooler region. This is a

very strange result. No one knows where the hotter or cooler regions are, but the researchers involved were convinced by the statistics that such regions do indeed exist. Unfortunately, this is the way that science is increasingly being conducted.

To confirm the temperature fluctuations allegedly discovered by COBE, the WMAP satellite was designed and then launched early in the 21st century. WMAP stands for the Wilkinson Microwave Anisotropy Probe, and was originally designated MAP, but was renamed after David Wilkinson, one of the main designers of the mission, died while the mission was underway. WMAP was constructed to detect the faint temperature variations indicated by COBE, and WMAP did confirm those fluctuations. In early 2003 a research team used the first WMAP results along with other data to establish some of the latest measurements of the universe. This study produced a 13.7 billion year age for the universe, plus or minus 1%. It also determined that visible matter accounts for only a little more than 4% of the mass of the universe. Of the remaining mass, some 23% is in the form of dark matter, with the remainder 73% in an exotic new form dubbed "dark energy." Dark energy will be described shortly.

THE HUBBLE CONSTANT

In the first chapter we saw that Hubble's original measurement of H_0 was greater than 500 km/sec Mpc, but that the value of H_0 had fallen to 50 km/sec Mpc by 1960. The value of H_0 remained there for more than three decades. In the early 1990's new studies suggested that H_0 should

Cosmic Strings

A brief mention should be made of cosmic strings, which must not be confused with the string theory of particles. Surveys of galaxies and clusters of galaxies show that they are not uniformly distributed. Instead, clusters of galaxies tend to lie along long, interconnected strands. If galaxies and other structures of the universe condensed around points that had greater than average mass and thus acted as gravitational seeds, then why are galaxies now found along long arcs? One possible answer is cosmic strings. Cosmic strings are hypothesized structures that stretch over vast distances in the universe. The strings are extremely thin but very long, and they contain incredible mass densities along their extent. Obviously cosmic strings are not made of "normal" matter. Cosmic strings were to act as gravitational seeds around which galaxies and clusters formed. There is yet no evidence of cosmic strings, and so this idea remains controversial.

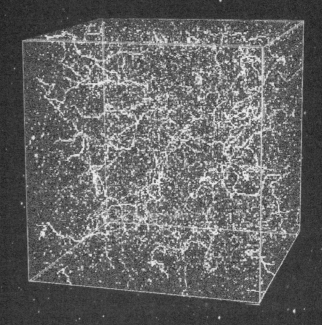

be closer to 80 km/sec. Astronomers who had for years supported the older value of H_0 strongly attacked the new value, and so there was much conflict on this issue for several years.

Besides professional pride, what else was at stake here? Not only can the Hubble constant give us the distance of galaxies, it can be used to find the approximate age of the universe. The inverse of the Hubble constant, T_H, is called the Hubble time, and it tells us how long ago the big bang was, assuming that Λ is zero and neglecting any decrease in the expansion due to the self-grav-

ity of matter in the universe. Since the universe must have undergone some sort of gravitational deceleration, the Hubble time is an upper limit to the age of a big-bang universe. If you examine the units of H_0 you will see that it has the dimensions of distance over time and distance so that the distances cancel and you are left with inverse time. Therefore T_H has the units of time, but the Mpc must be converted to kilometers and the seconds should be converted to years.

For instance, a Hubble constant of 50 km/sec Mpc gives a T_H of 1/50 Mpc sec/km. A parsec

contains 3×10^{13} km, so an Mpc equals 3×10^{19} km. A year has approximately 3×10^7 seconds. Putting this together we get

$$T_H = (1/50 \text{ Mpc sec/km})(3 \times 10^{19} \text{ km/Mpc})(\text{year}/3 \times 10^7 \text{ sec}) = 2 \times 10^{10} \text{ years.}$$

Therefore a Hubble constant of 50 km/sec Mpc yields a Hubble time of 20 billion years. Factoring in a reasonable gravitational deceleration gives the oft-quoted age since the big bang of 16 to 18 billion years.

Since the Hubble time is inversely proportional to the Hubble constant, doubling H_0 would halve T_H. The suggestion that H_0 should be increased to 80 km/sec Mpc decreased the Hubble time to about 12.5 billion years. Gravitational deceleration would have decreased the actual age of the universe to as little as 8 billion years. This ordinarily could be accepted, except that astronomers were convinced that globular star clusters, which contain what are thought to be among the oldest stars in our galaxy, were close to 15 billion years old. Thus a higher Hubble constant would place astronomers in the embarrassing position of having stars older than the universe.

There were several possible ways to resolve this dilemma, and astronomers eventually settled upon a combination of two. First, the teams of astronomers who were championing different values for H_0 found some common ground and were able to reach a consensus between their two values. At the time of the writing of this book (2003) the established value for H_0 is 72 km/sec Mpc. This gives an age of the universe between 12 and 15 billion years, with the preferred value at the time of this writing as 13.7 billion years. Second, the ages of globular star clusters were reevaluated. We will not discuss how this was done in detail, but it involves properly calibrating color-magnitude diagrams of globular clusters. Calibration requires knowing the distance, and the Hubble Space Telescope provided new data that enabled us to more accurately know the distances of globular clusters. The recalibration reduced the ages of globular clusters to a range only slightly less than the new age of the universe. In the estimation of most cosmologists the uncertainty in both ages allows enough time for the formation of the earliest stars sometime after the big bang.

This episode does illustrate the changing nature of science and the unwarranted confidence that scientists often place in the thinking of the day. Before this crisis in the age of the universe and the ages of globular clusters, most astronomers were thoroughly convinced that both of these ages were correct. Anyone who had suggested that globular clusters were less than 15 billion years old would have been dismissed rather quickly. However when other data demanded a change, necessity as the mother of invention stepped in, and a way to reduce the ages of globular clusters was found. The absolute truth of the younger ages has now replaced the absolute truth of the older ages. What most scientists miss is that, apart from crises, the new truth would never have been discovered. We would have blithely gone on totally unaware that our "objective approach" to the ages of globular clusters had for a long time failed to give us the "correct" value.

THE RETURN OF THE COSMOLOGICAL CONSTANT

As discussed in chapter 1, Einstein had given a non-zero value to the cosmological constant to preserve a static universe, a move that he later regretted. For some time Λ equal to zero came into vogue, and many cosmologists frowned upon any suggestion otherwise. Actually the idea of non-zero Λ never really went away. For instance, by the 1950s many geologists were insisting that the age of the earth was close to the currently accepted value of 4.6 billion years, but the Hubble constant of the day was far too large to permit the universe to be this old. Some cosmologists proposed that a large Λ had increased the rate of expansion in the past so that the corresponding Hubble time gave a false indication of the true age of the universe. Just as gravitational deceleration can cause the actual age of the universe to be far less than the Hubble time, an acceleration powered by Λ can cause the actual age of the universe to be greater than the Hubble time. In the mid 1950s the cosmological distance scale was revised in such a fashion that the Hubble constant was decreased to pretty much what it is today with a corresponding increase in the Hubble time so as to produce a universe much older than 4.6 billion years. Therefore there did not seem to be much need for a non-zero Λ.

After four decades of smugness, Λ has made a comeback. In 1998 some very subtle cosmological studies using distances from type Ia supernovae and linking several parameters of the universe suggested that the best fit to the data is that Λ has a small non-zero value. Since its reemergence astronomers have begun to call the cosmological constant "dark energy." The cosmological constant corresponds to energy, because it does represent a repulsive force, and such forces always can be written as a potential energy. Einstein showed that energy and mass are equivalent, so cosmic repulsion can be viewed similarly to mass. Since neither cosmic repulsion nor dark matter can be seen, and since both critically affect the structure of the universe, it is appropriate to view the two in a similar way. As uncomfortable as this may be for some, cosmologists have been forced to reconsider the cosmological constant. Where this will lead is not known at the time of this writing.

The value of Λ has ramifications in the future of the universe. In most discussions of cosmology, the future of the universe is tied to the geometry of the universe. These discussions are based upon the model developed by the Russian mathematician Alexandre Friedman in 1922, a model that is called the Friedman universe. The Friedman universe supposes that the value of Λ is zero. In the Friedman model, if the average density of the universe is below some critical density, then the universe is spatially infinite and it will expand forever. This corresponds to negative curvature where there are an infinite number of lines through a point that are parallel to any other line. If the average density of the universe is above the critical density, then the universe is spatially finite, though it is not bound. This universe will eventually cease expanding and reverse in a contraction. The geometry of this universe has positive curvature so that there are no

parallel lines. The critical density depends upon the Hubble constant. The currently accepted value of the Hubble constant results in a critical density that is higher than the density of lighted matter in the universe. Dark matter and dark energy bring the total density of the universe very close to the critical density, though no one expects it to exceed the critical density.

A universe that will expand forever is said to be open, while a universe that will cease expanding is called closed. Technically, the terms open and closed actually refer to the geometry of the universe, but with a Friedman universe they may refer to the ultimate fate of the universe as well. However, when Λ is not zero this relationship is altered. In such a universe, the open or closed status of the universe directly refers to the geometry via the density. For instance, a closed universe could expand forever. This is a fine point that many books on cosmology get wrong, because they only consider Friedman models. For many years only Friedman models were seriously considered. Since 1998 non-Friedman models have dominated cosmological thinking and with time this fine point will probably work its way into many books about cosmology.

THE ORIGIN OF THE UNIVERSE

The origin of the universe is a mysterious topic. For instance, the sudden appearance of matter and energy would seem to violate the conservation of energy (the first law of thermodynamics) and matter. Science is based upon what we can observe. Regardless of how or when the universe came into being, it was an event that happened only once in time (as we know time). No human being was present at the beginning of the universe, so one would expect that the origin of the universe is not a scientific question at all, but that has not kept scientists from asking whence came the big bang. As discussed further in the next chapter, some Christian apologists see in the big bang evidence of God's existence. Their reasoning is that something cannot come from nothing, and so there must be a Creator. Cosmologists are well aware of this dilemma, and they have offered several theoretical scenarios whereby the universe could have come into existence without an external agent.

One proposal originally offered by Edward Tryon in 1973 is that the universe came about through what is called a quantum fluctuation. As discussed in the beginning of chapter 1, quantum mechanics tells us that particles have a wave nature, and thus there is a fundamental uncertainty that is significant in the microscopic world. By its very nature a wave is spread out so that one cannot definitely assign a location to the wave. Usually this principle is called the Heisenberg uncertainty principle, named for the German physicist who first deduced it. The uncertainty principle can be stated a couple of different ways. One statement involves the uncertainty in a particle's position and the uncertainty of a particle's momentum. Momentum is the product of a particle's mass and velocity. Whenever we measure anything, there is uncertainty in the measurement. The Heisenberg uncertainty principle states that the product of the uncertainty in a particle's position and the uncertainty in a particle's momentum must be no less than a certain fundamental constant.

In mathematical form this formulation of the uncertainty principle appears as

$$\Delta x \, \Delta p \geq \hbar /2$$

where Δx is the uncertainty in the position of a particle and Δp is the uncertainty in the momentum of a particle. The fundamental constant is $\hbar$, called h-bar, and is equal to 1.055×10^{-34} joule-second.

What the uncertainty principle means is that the more accurately that we know one quantity (the lower that its uncertainty is), the less accurately we know the other quantity (the greater that its uncertainty is). If we measure the position of a small particle such as an electron very precisely, then we know very little about the particle's momentum. Since we know the mass of an electron pretty well, the uncertainty in the momentum is mostly due to our ignorance of the electron's speed. If on the other hand we know the particle's speed to a high degree of accuracy, we will not know the particle's position very well. Recall from the discussion in chapter 1 that this is a fundamental uncertainty, and not merely a limitation imposed by our measuring techniques. That is, even if we had infinite precision in our measuring techniques, we would still have the limitation of the uncertainty principle.

This behavior seems rather bizarre, because it is not encountered in everyday experience. The reason is that the wavelengths of large objects are so small that we cannot see the wave nature of macroscopic objects. Another way of looking at it is that $\hbar$ is very small, so small that the uncertainties in position and momentum of macroscopic systems is completely dwarfed by macroscopic errors in measurement totally unrelated to the uncertainty principle. Therefore while the uncertainty principle applies to all systems, its effects are noticeable only in very small systems where the value of $\hbar$ is comparable to the properties of the objects involved. As bizarre as the uncertainty principle may seem, it has been confirmed in a number of experiments.

Another statement of the uncertainty principle involves the uncertainty in measuring a particle's energy and the uncertainty in the time required to conduct the experiment. In mathematical form this statement is

$$\Delta E \, \Delta t \geq \hbar /2$$

where ΔE is the uncertainty in the energy and Δt is the uncertainty in the time. Basically this statement means that we can measure the energy of a microscopic system with some precision or we can measure the time of the measurement with some precision, but we cannot measure both with great precision simultaneously.

One application of this statement of the uncertainty principle is a process whereby a pair of virtual particles can be produced. The conservation of mass and energy (they are related through Einstein's famous equation $E = mc^2$) seems to prevent the spontaneous appearance of particles out of nothing. However, there is nothing else that prevents this from happening, and the uncertainty principle offers a way to get around this objection, if for only a short period of time. For instance, in empty space an electron and its anti-particle, the positron, can spontaneously form. This would introduce a violation of the conservation of energy, ΔE. Being anti-particles, the electron and positron have opposite charges so that they attract one another. As the two particles come into contact they are annihilated and release the same amount of energy that was required to create them. The energy conservation violation that occurred when the particle pair formed is exactly cancelled by the energy released when the particles annihilate. That is, there is no net change in the energy of the universe. As long as the particle pair exists for a short enough period of time, Δt, so that the product of ΔE and Δt does not violate the uncertainty principle, then this brief trifling violation of the conservation of energy/mass can occur. Such matters are called quantum fluctuations. A number of quantum mechanical effects have been interpreted as manifestations of quantum fluctuations.

Larger violations of the conservation of energy cannot exist for as long a time interval as smaller violations. For example, since protons have nearly 2,000 times as much mass (and hence energy) as electrons, proton/anti-proton pairs produced this way can last for no more than 1/2,000 as long as pairs of electrons and positrons created by pair production. A macroscopic violation of the conservation of energy would last for such a short length of time that it cannot be observed. However, what would happen if a macroscopic

phenomenon had exactly zero energy? To be more specific, suppose that the universe has total energy equal to zero? Then the universe could have come into existence and lasted for a very long period of time, because if ΔE is zero, Δt can have any finite value and still satisfy the uncertainty principle. Therefore the universe could have come into existence without violating the conservation of energy. If this were true, then the universe is no more than a quantum fluctuation.

The trick is to find some way to make the sum total of energy in the universe equal to zero. The universe obviously contains much energy in the form of matter ($E = mc^2$) and radiant energy (photons of all wavelengths), as well as more exotic particles such as neutrinos. There are forms of negative energy that many cosmologists think may balance all of this positive energy. The most obvious choice for this negative energy is gravitational potential energy. The gravitational potential energy for a particle near a large mass has the form

$$E = -GmM/r$$

where G is the universal gravitational constant, m is the mass of the particle, M is the mass of the large mass, and r is the distance of the particle from the large mass. This equation could be summed over all of the mass of the universe to obtain the total gravitational potential energy of the universe. Since the gravitational potential energy has a negative sign, all terms would be negative, and the sum must be negative as well. Therefore it is reasoned that the gravitational potential energy could exactly equal the total positive energy so that the total energy of the universe is zero.

However there are at least a couple of problems with this. First, we do not know the variables involved well enough to properly evaluate the energies to determine if indeed the energy of the universe is zero. Therefore it is more a matter of faith that the sum of the energy of the universe is zero. A second, more difficult, problem is with the negative sign in the gravitational potential energy equation. The sign appears because the reference point is taken at infinity. All potential energies require the selection of an arbitrary reference point where the potential energy is zero. The reference point for gravity is taken at infinity for mathematical simplicity. This forces all gravitational potential energies at finite distances to be negative. Any other zero point could be chosen, though that would make the mathematics more complicated. Any other reference point would make at least some of the gravitational potential energies positive. Alternately, one could add an arbitrary constant to the potential energy term, because the zero point is arbitrary. This is true for all potential energies. In other words, one cannot honestly state that the gravitational potential energy of the universe has any particular value to balance other forms of energy.

In his original 1973 paper on the quantum fluctuation theory for the origin of the big bang, Edward Tryon stated, "I offer the modest proposal that our universe is simply one of those things which happen from time to time." Alan Guth has echoed this sentiment with the observation that the whole universe may be "a free lunch." Indeed, Guth's inflationary model depends upon a quantum fluctuation as the origin of the big bang. In the inflationary model the universe sprang from a quantum fluctuation that was a "false vacuum," an entity predicted by some particle physicists, but never observed. While a true vacuum is ostensibly empty, it can give rise to ghostly particles through pair production. On the other hand, a false vacuum can do this and more. A false vacuum would have a strong repulsive gravitational field that would explosively expand the early universe. Another peculiarity of a false vacuum is that it would maintain a constant energy density as it expands, creating vast amounts of energy more or less out of nothing.

The quantum fluctuation theory of the origin of the universe has been expanded upon to allow for many other universes. In this view the universe did not arise as a quantum fluctuation *ex nihilo*, but instead arose as a quantum fluctuation in some other universe. A small quantum fluctuation in that universe immediately divorced itself from that universe to become ours. Presumably that universe also arose from a quantum fluctuation in a previous universe. Perhaps our universe is frequently giving birth to new universes in a similar fashion. This long chain of an infinite number of universes is a sort of return to the eternal universe, though any particular universe such as ours may have a finite lifetime. This idea is the multi-verse mentioned earlier that has been invoked to explain the anthropic principle. In each universe one would expect that the physical constants would be different. Only in a universe where the constants are conducive for life would cognizant beings exist to take note of such things. Thus, selection of universes in which we could exist might be limited.

Some cosmologists have suggested an oscillating universe to explain the origin of the universe. In this view, the mass density of the universe is sufficient to slow and then reverse the expansion of the universe. This would lead to the "big crunch" mentioned earlier. After the big crunch, the universe would "bounce" and be reborn as another big bang. This big bang would be followed by another big crunch, which would repeat in an infinite cycle. Therefore, our finite-age universe would merely be a single episode of an eternal oscillating universe. Some have fantasized that the laws of physics may be juggled between each rebirth.

There are several things wrong with the oscillating universe. First, the best evidence today suggests that Ω is too small to halt the expansion of the universe. Second, even if the universe were destined to someday contract, there is no known mechanism that would cause it to bounce. We would expect that once the universe imploded upon itself, it would remain as some sort of black-hole sort of state (incidentally, if the big bang started in this sort of state, then this would be a problem for the single big-bang model as well). Third, there is no way that we can test this, so it is hardly a scientific concept.

One last attempt to explain the beginning (or non-beginning) of the universe should be mentioned. If the universe is infinite in size, then it has always been and always will be infinite in size. As the universe expands, it becomes larger and cooler, and its density decreases. What if the universe has been expanding forever? One possibility is that the physical laws that govern the universe change as the average temperature changes. This is the essence of GUT described earlier. Most physicists think that the fundamental forces that we observe today are different manifestations of a single force that has had its symmetry broken. Perhaps in much earlier times when the universe was much hotter and denser, other laws of physics totally unknowable to us were in effect. If this were true, then what we call the big bang was just a transition from a much higher density and temperature state. The big bang would have been some sort of wall beyond which we cannot penetrate to earlier times with our physics. Before the big bang the universe would have contained unbelievable densities and temperatures, and the physical laws would have been quite foreign to us. Thus the universe has always been expanding through various transitions, and there is no ultimate beginning to explain. This, too, represents a return to the eternal universe that the big bang was long thought to have eliminated.

Big-bang research of recent years has been in the direction of explaining the origin of the universe in an entirely physical, natural way without recourse to a Creator. Any purely physical explanation of origins without a Creator amounts to non-theistic evolution, naturalism, and secular humanism. All these ideas are antithetical to biblical Christianity. Those Christian apologists who fail to see this simply have failed to understand the direction that cosmology has taken in recent years.

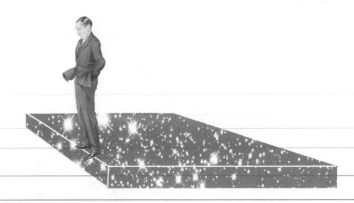

CHECKING YOUR UNDERSTANDING

1. What is the flatness problem?

2. What is the anthropic principle?

3. What is inflation?

4. What is dark matter?

5. What did the COBE and WMAP missions find?

6. What is dark energy?

7. What is the Hubble time?

8. What are some ways that cosmologists have suggested that the universe began?

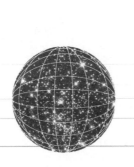

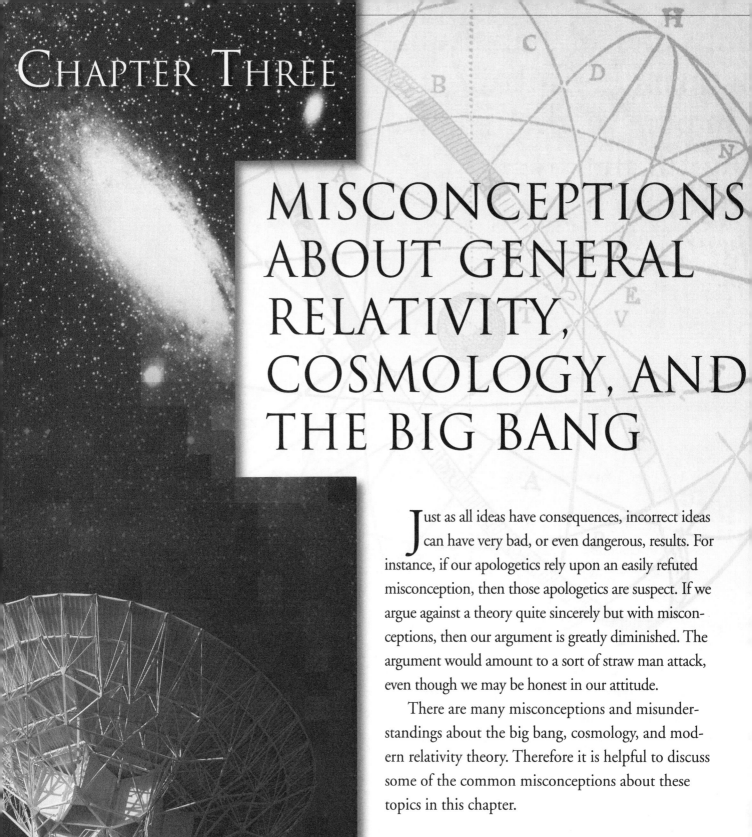

CHAPTER THREE

MISCONCEPTIONS ABOUT GENERAL RELATIVITY, COSMOLOGY, AND THE BIG BANG

Just as all ideas have consequences, incorrect ideas can have very bad, or even dangerous, results. For instance, if our apologetics rely upon an easily refuted misconception, then those apologetics are suspect. If we argue against a theory quite sincerely but with misconceptions, then our argument is greatly diminished. The argument would amount to a sort of straw man attack, even though we may be honest in our attitude.

There are many misconceptions and misunderstandings about the big bang, cosmology, and modern relativity theory. Therefore it is helpful to discuss some of the common misconceptions about these topics in this chapter.

THE REDSHIFT IS NOT A DOPPLER SHIFT

In describing the expansion of the universe, most treatments compare the redshifts of universal expansion to Doppler shifts. The Doppler shift is named for Christian Doppler, who discovered the principle in 1842. This phenomenon occurs with all waves, such as sound waves from a car horn. If the horn of an approaching car is sounded, adjacent sound waves will be crammed closer together so that we encounter more waves per second than if the car were not moving with respect to us. More waves per second correspond to an increase in frequency. Since our ears detect frequency as pitch, the increased frequency results in higher pitch than what we would hear from a stationary car. If the car is moving away from us, the waves are stretched so that we encounter a lower frequency, and we hear a lower pitch. If the car remains motionless and the listener moves toward or away from the car instead, then the pitch is increased or decreased in a similar fashion.

The light from stars can be Doppler shifted as well. If we move toward a star or it moves toward us, all of the star's light will be shifted toward shorter wavelengths. Light is perceived as color, the shorter wavelengths being toward the blue end of the spectrum. Therefore we say that the star's light is Doppler shifted toward the blue. On the other hand, if a star moves away from us or we move away from the star, the star's light is Doppler shifted toward longer wavelengths, and we say that the star's light is shifted toward the red. With either a blue or red Doppler shift, the entire spectrum of the star is shifted. The spectra of stars contain dark absorption lines. (please see the appendix for an explanation of how spectral lines are formed). Due to the Doppler effect, spectral lines will be slightly shifted from the wavelengths that they usually have. The amount of Doppler shift is measured by the displacement of these lines, and the amount of relative velocity can be calculated using an equation called the Doppler formula.

A star's Doppler motion is a combination of our motion through space and the star's motion. Through careful analysis of the Doppler motions of thousands of stars, astronomers have been able to determine roughly what our motion through space is. In turn, we have been able to measure the motions of individual stars in space. For instance, we know that the sun is moving nearly 250 km/sec as it orbits the center of the galaxy. We have found that stars generally follow one of two very different kinds of orbits around the galaxy, and these two types of orbits manifest themselves as different speeds. There are other subtle differences between these two groups of stars, which has become the basis of stellar population types.[1]

It is very easy to visualize the expansion of the universe as matter flying apart in space; so most books on the subject use the Doppler shift as the explanation of what is happening. This is most unfortunate, because this is not what is actually happening. Cosmologists usually assume that all matter in the universe is at rest with respect to space. What is expanding is space itself. Therefore, as space expands, the matter in the universe is carried along with the expansion. As such, particles are not actually moving apart. Instead, more space appears between particles as the universe expands.

A balloon is often used as a two-dimensional example of the expanding universe. If dots are placed on the balloon with a marking pen, the dots will appear to move apart as the balloon is blown up. However the dots will grow in size with the expanding balloon, which is not what objects in the universe do. A better analogy is to glue sequins on the balloon. The sequins will appear to move apart, but the sequins themselves will not increase in size as the balloon expands. Notice that the sequins are not actually moving, but simply appear to move

A balloon is often used as a two-dimensional example of the expanding universe.

apart as they are carried along by the expansion of the balloon. In like fashion, galaxies can be at rest with respect to space, but they appear to fly apart due to the expansion of space. Therefore the redshifts due to the expansion of the universe are not Doppler shifts. Sometimes the perceived motion due to expansion is called Hubble flow.

This may seem like a minor distinction, but missing this very subtle point can lead to major misunderstandings. For example, the spectrum of the Andromeda Galaxy (M31) is blue shifted. Some ask how this can be, if the universe is expanding. Virtually all galaxies are in fact moving through space, rather than being at rest as in the very simple view mentioned above. What is the source of this motion? In most cases it is probably due to local gravity. Galaxies tend to clump together into clusters containing anywhere between a few dozen to a thousand galaxies. Our galaxy is a member of an assembly of about 30 galaxies called the Local Group, which happens to lie near the much larger Virgo Cluster. Clusters of clusters may form larger structures called super clusters.

All of these structures are presumably held together by gravity, which would imply that the various objects making them up have orbits. These orbital motions produce relative motions that are indeed Doppler in nature. Therefore the spectrum of any particular galaxy will have shifts due to the Doppler effect and Hubble flow at the same time. Since there is no way to observationally distinguish the two, we cannot say for sure how much of each exists. M31 is so close to us that its Hubble flow would amount to no more than 50 km/sec. Its gravitational motion greatly exceeds this, so the Doppler effect dominates the spectral shift of M31. The Doppler motion of M31 happens to be toward us. A few other galaxies show blue shifts, and they are all very close to us as well.

The mixing of Hubble flow and Doppler motion presents a problem in measuring the Hubble constant. To accurately measure the Hubble constant, we must sample galaxies that have large Hubble flows as compared to their Doppler motions. Doppler motions should be independent of distance, but Hubble flow must be proportional to distance (this is the Hubble relation). Nearby galaxies can best have their distances measured, but their shifts are dominated by Doppler motion. More distant galaxies have spectral shifts that are dominated by Hubble flow, but their distances are more difficult to measure accurately. Separating the two effects requires that we make certain assumptions and handle the data in particular ways. Part of the disagreement over the value of the Hubble constant in recent years has resulted from different approaches in handling this problem.

A FEW BLUESHIFTED GALAXIES ARE NOT A PROBLEM FOR THE EXPANDING UNIVERSE

As mentioned in the previous section, the Andromeda Galaxy has a blueshift rather than a redshift. This means that this galaxy is moving toward us rather than away from us. Some think that this is a problem for an expanding universe, thinking that in an expanding universe all galaxies must have redshifts. However, motions of nearby galaxies due to local gravity can overtake the expansion of the universe. Note that this can be true only of nearby galaxies. If a distant galaxy were to be found to have a blueshift, that would be a problem for the expanding universe.

On a related issue, about half the stars within our galaxy have redshift, while the other half have blueshift. Some people think that any object with a blueshift is a problem with an expanding universe. However, the effect of universal expansion is extremely small on the local scale. For instance, people on the other side of the earth are not getting farther from you because of expansion. Local effects, primarily gravity, overcome the extremely feeble universal expansion. Within our galaxy, gravity is the dominant force that holds the galaxy together. The blueshifts and redshifts that we observe in stars within our galaxy are due to Doppler shifts resulting from the orbits of the sun and the other stars around the galaxy. So this is not a problem for an expanding universe.

INFLATION DOES NOT CONTRADICT THE PROHIBITION OF FASTER-THAN-LIGHT SPEED

As previously discussed, physicists believe that faster-than-light speed is not possible. Because of mass increases with increasing speed, a particle that has mass would have infinite mass at the speed of light. Therefore, to accelerate a particle to the speed of light, an infinite amount of energy would be required. Since we do not have an infinite amount of energy at our disposal, no material particle can travel with the speed of light, though the speed may be arbitrarily close to the speed of light.

Because of this speed limit imposed upon matter, many people think that the faster-than-light expansion of inflationary cosmologies is not possible. If the expansion of the universe were due to Doppler motion, then this would be a problem. However, as discussed earlier, Hubble flow and Doppler motions are different. During an episode of inflation, particles do separate much faster than the speed of light, but that separation is not due to the motions of the particles through space, but by the rapid stretching of the space between the particles. This is a good example of how misunderstanding a concept can lead to erroneous conclusions.

INTERSTELLAR REDDENING IS NOT THE SAME AS A REDSHIFT

Like other spiral galaxies, the disk of the Milky Way contains a huge amount of dust. Dust particles are called grains, and are typically about 0.1 micron in size. Dust grains are probably made of a variety of substances, including silicates, carbon, iron, and ices. Dust tends to clump, so that there are regions in the disk of the galaxy that are pretty dust free, while other regions are extremely dusty. As starlight passes through dust, the grains scatter the light. The size of dust grains favors the scattering of shorter wavelengths (blue) of light more than longer wavelengths (red). The solid particles in cigarette smoke are about the same size, so that they also scatter blue light more effectively. That is why cigarette smoke appears blue when illuminated by strong light. Molecules in the earth's atmosphere preferentially scatter sunlight in much the same way to produce the familiar blue sky.

When light is scattered, it is removed from the transmitted light. Some of the red light is scattered, but not as much as blue light is. Therefore, if light that has undergone scattering is observed, it will appear both fainter and redder. This is the reason why the rising or setting sun appears much dimmer and redder than the sun does high in the sky. At those times the light from the sun is entering the earth's atmosphere at a grazing angle so that it passes through much more air than when the sun is higher in the sky. More air results in more scattering, making the sun appear simultaneously fainter and redder. Starlight undergoes much the same thing. The light from more distant stars generally must pass through more dust than the light from nearer stars, so more distant stars appear fainter and redder than they normally would. The reddening of starlight is called interstellar reddening, and the dimming of starlight is called extinction. In calculating distances of astronomical bodies, a correction for extinction must be applied.

Some people confuse interstellar reddening and redshift. The redshift changes all wavelengths of light by the same relative amount. The shape of the spectrum, often closely approximating what is called a blackbody, is preserved. All spectral lines are shifted by the same relative amount, which allows us to measure the amount of redshift. Interstellar reddening does not shift wavelengths — all spectral lines remain at where they normally would occur. The entire spectrum is depressed, and since the blue end of the spectrum is depressed more than the red end, the shape of the spectrum is altered.

THE REDSHIFT DOES NOT USUALLY MAKE GALAXIES APPEAR RED

Some people have the impression that redshift makes galaxies appear more red in color. For most galaxies the redshift is so small that there is no appreciable change in color. Even for galaxies with large redshifts, the color of the galaxies will not be changed much. The reason is that although visible light from a galaxy is shifted to longer wavelengths and even into the infrared that the eye cannot see, that light is approximately replaced with normally invisible radiation in the ultraviolet that is shifted into the visible part of the spectrum. Therefore the spectrum of a galaxy has about the same shape as it would have if it had no redshift, and so the color is about the same.

With very large redshift, the color of a galaxy is altered so that the galaxy is redder than it normally would be, but the eye cannot detect this subtle color change. This color change can be determined by comparing the brightness of a galaxy at two different wavelengths, for instance in blue and yellow light. From the study of many nearby galaxies we have a good idea of what color a typical galaxy has. Very high redshift galaxies have systematically redder colors as determined with this method.

This process can be used to advantage in estimating redshifts. Taking photographs is a very efficient use of light, while spectroscopy is very inefficient. The difference occurs because with spectroscopy the light must be dispersed, or spread out. Observing time on very large telescopes is valuable, so we do not want to waste time measuring every galaxy for its redshift. Instead, in searching for distant galaxies we would like to select for spectroscopy those galaxies that likely have large redshifts. Measuring their colors may identify likely candidates for further study. Sometimes galaxies near the limit of detectability have been photographed, such as in the Hubble deep sky field (see photo next

Hubble deep sky field

page). These galaxies are so faint that their spectra cannot be measured, but astronomers can estimate the amount of redshift from the colors. A correction must be applied, because astronomers expect that very distant galaxies are bluer than nearby galaxies. This is because astronomers assume that the light from very great distances originated when the sources were much younger. Galaxies in their youth are supposed to be dominated by blue light, because astronomers think that massive blue stars dominated the first generations of stars.

MODERN RELATIVITY THEORY DOES NOT ELIMINATE THE CONCEPT OF AN ABSOLUTE REFERENCE FRAME

This is probably the most misunderstood aspect of modern relativity. Newton had formulated his laws with the assumption that there was some absolute standard of rest from which all motion could be measured. This eventually led to the development of the idea of aether, the stuff of space. Maxwell's theory of electricity and magnetism developed in the 1860s suggested that light was a wave in this aether. The 1887 Michelson-Morley experiment was an attempt to measure the motion of the earth through the aether as it orbited the sun. The Michelson-Morley experiment was a null result, suggesting that the earth was not moving with respect to the aether or if you will, space. However, annually varying Doppler shifts in the spectra of stars as the earth orbited the sun strongly suggested that the earth was indeed moving. How this discrepancy could be explained remained a mystery for nearly two decades.

Albert Einstein pursued another explanation of the problem in his 1905 paper on special relativity. Einstein assumed that physical laws and the speed of light were invariant with speed. That is, no matter what one's speed is, physical laws and the speed of light would be the same. Classical physics assumes that while physical laws are not changed by one's speed, the observed speed of light should be the vector sum of one's velocity and the velocity of light. Therefore if one measured the speed of an oncoming light beam as we moved toward the beam, the measured speed of light ought to be c + v, where c is the speed of light in the absence of our motion, and v is our speed. If on the other hand we are moving in the direction in which the light beam is traveling, we would expect to measure the speed of light to be c − v. The Michelson-Morley experiment revealed that the answer was c in either case. Einstein took this fact as a given.

With this novel, if not counterintuitive, assumption Einstein worked out the implications. He showed that as an object's speed increases, its mass increases, its length decreases, and time in the reference frame of the moving object is slowed with respect to a reference frame that is not moving. Each of these effects has subsequently been confirmed with numerous experiments, mostly dealing with fast-moving elementary particles. For instance, unstable elementary particles that rapidly decay last longer when moving at high speeds. Another example is the observed increase in the masses of particles in particle accelerators. The mass increases limit the highest speeds that can be attained with a type of particle accelerator called the cyclotron.

The early success of special relativity was hailed as the end of the aether. Many scientists at the time claimed the concept of absolute space was no longer tenable. Even an early quote by Einstein suggested that he shared this belief. A decade after his paper on special relativity, Einstein published his general relativity that addressed accelerated reference frames and provided a new theory of gravity. Special relativity had considered only constantly moving reference frames, so a new theory had to be developed to handle ones that were changing speeds. One consequence of his theory was that a constantly accelerated frame is not distinguishable from a gravitational field. This ultimately led to the new approach to gravity, as discussed in chapter 1.

The early rejection of the concept of the aether or an absolute reference frame gave rise to the twin paradox, another idea that is frequently mishandled. Suppose that there are identical twin brothers. At about age 20 one twin goes on a voyage to a nearby star system at nearly the speed of light, while the other remains back on earth. After 40 years have passed on earth, the astronaut returns. The twin that remained on earth is now 60 years old and is showing his age, but due to time dilation the astronaut has only experienced a few months aging and looks pretty much the same as when he left earth. The astronaut has moved at a high speed compared to his brother on earth and so time has passed more slowly.

The paradox comes in when one considers the reference frame of the astronaut. If all reference frames are equal, as is allegedly what relativity theory says, then from the reference frame of the astronaut, his brother on the earth is the one that has moved, not the astronaut. This would suggest that the twin on earth should have experienced less time than the astronaut did. In other words, each twin could claim that the other one did the moving and hence experienced time dilation. Since both twins could not have undergone time dilation, the twin paradox is thought by some to invalidate relativity theory.

If all we had was special relativity, then the twin paradox might be a serious problem. However, we do have general relativity, which addresses accelerated reference frames. The astronaut twin had to undergo four separate accelerations. The first was to achieve a high speed in the first place. The second was to slow down upon reaching his destination. The third and fourth would have occurred upon starting the return journey to earth and slowing down to arrive at the earth. Meanwhile the twin on earth experienced no accelerations relevant to the problem. How do we measure accelerations? Accelerations can be measured with respect to the sum total of the matter of the universe. Upon acceleration, someone can observe that his speed is changing with respect to distant massive objects such as stars and galaxies. The earth-bound twin does not see this effect of acceleration, while his astronaut brother does. Therefore we can unambiguously determine which twin does the moving, and the twin paradox dissolves away.

The ability to measure accelerations with respect to distant massive objects is called Mach's principle. Mach's principle applies to constant motion as well. While individual distant massive objects may have their own motions, the sum total of all the matter in the universe is believed to be at rest with respect to space. Therefore the sum total of matter in the universe represents a preferred standard of rest. Early in the 20th century, some theorists stated the modern relativity theory demands that there is no preferred standard of rest, that is, that all non-accelerated frames of reference are equally valid. This idea has become a common popular belief. However, this is in direct conflict with Mach's principle, a foundation of modern relativity theory. So contrary to those early pronouncements and the public's conception, modern relativity theory does tell us that there is an absolute standard of rest. That standard of rest is the frame of reference that is at rest with respect to the sum of all distant objects. Keep in mind that general relativity holds that space is a thing. One could argue that space as understood by general relativity could be identified with an aether, albeit not in the form originally envisioned.

THE CONSTANCY IN THE SPEED OF LIGHT IS MISUNDERSTOOD

One of the foundations of special and general relativity is that the speed of light is a constant, regardless of the speed of the source or the observer. As discussed in the previous section, this is very different from what one might expect. Unfortunately, many people misunderstand this principle. When light enters a medium, such as glass, the speed decreases. To many people this seems to violate the principle that the speed of light is a constant. However, the constancy of the speed of light refers to the measured speed with regard to the motion of the source and observer. The speed of light has its greatest value in a vacuum, and all speeds in media are less than the vacuum speed. Within a medium, the constancy of the speed of light regardless of the motions of the source and observer is true.

A few years ago scientists measured the speed of light in a particular form of matter called a Bose-Einstein condensate to be a mere 17 m/sec. This speed is so incredibly slow that many people thought that this just had to violate the constancy of the speed of light, but this is not the case. Some asked if this means that light in some medium could travel faster than the speed of light in a vacuum. Theoretically this is not the case, and

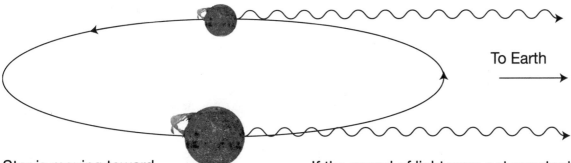

Star is moving away from Earth at velocity V.

If the speed of light were not constant, the light from this star would travel at velocity C - V.

To Earth

Star is moving toward Earth at velocity V.

If the speed of light were not constant, the light from this star would travel at velocity C + V and would reach Earth sooner.

measurements of light speed in all media so far confirm that.

There have been experiments in recent years that have suggested to some physicists that the speed of light in some situations has been greater than the theoretical maximum of 300,000 km/s. These experiments and their interpretation have been very controversial. There are explanations that do not require supraliminal light speed. Until the physics community has fully digested this, it is not possible to discuss this issue further.

ACCEPTANCE OF GENERAL RELATIVITY DOES NOT AMOUNT TO ACCEPTANCE OF MORAL RELATIVISM

Soon after the publication of Einstein's theories of relativity early in the 20th century, moral relativists seized upon the theories as support for their philosophy. They peddled the idea that all morals and standards were relative, so no standard could be held to be absolute. Moral relativists continued to spread the myth that Einstein's theories of relativity proved that there were no absolute standards, but only relative ones. As shown in an earlier section, this assertion is patently false. Einstein himself did not like the name "relativity," but instead called his theory, the "theory of invariance." If anything, even special relativity alone posits that there is at least one absolute, the speed of light. A key foundation of general relativity is Mach's principle, which states that there is an absolute standard of space against which all motions may be measured.

There is also the question of how a theory about the physical world could establish the basis of a system of morality. This is a gigantic leap of logic that was never demonstrated. The misappropriation of Einstein's relativity theory by moral relativists ought to be opposed. Unfortunately, many Christians have allowed this fraud to continue or even unwittingly participated in it by arguing against relativity theory on similar philosophical grounds.

THE BIG BANG WAS NOT AN EXPLOSION

The name "big bang" is a misnomer. As mentioned in a previous chapter, Sir Fred Hoyle, who meant it as a term of derision, inadvertently coined the name. Unfortunately, to many people the name suggests an explosion. For instance, some critics ask the question, "What exploded?" To add to this, many popular accounts discuss the big bang as if it were an explosion. Explosions tend to be catastrophic events that lead to chaos and disorder, so the question is often asked how an explosion could have led to the order that we see in the universe. However, the only similarity between the big bang and an explosion is the sudden appearance of the universe and the resulting expansion of matter and energy. A true explosion would produce Doppler motion, but universal expansion is different from Doppler motion, as previously discussed.

For some time the model of the big bang has not been one of an explosion, so it is very important for critics of the big-bang theory that we correctly state the model so that we cannot stand accused of using a straw man argument. The universe is supposed to have begun in a high-temperature, high-density, but very uniform state. Uniformity is hardly the description of an explosion – an explosion should have introduced non-uniformity at its inception. Through expansion the density and temperature of the universe would have decreased to their current values. The uniformity of the universe must have been preserved through much of the expansion. The universe today is not uniform, so how did the universe develop non-uniformity? This is a bit of a problem for the big-bang model today, a topic that will be further explored in the next chapter.

THE UNIVERSE IS NOT EXPANDING INTO ANYTHING

A frequent criticism of the expanding universe is to ask, "What is the universe expanding into?" The simple answer is that the universe is not expanding into anything. This misconception probably stems from the common analogy made to an expanding balloon, as discussed earlier in this chapter. As the balloon expands, spots on the balloon move apart. This two-dimensional analogy shows rather nicely how objects in the three-dimensional universe can get farther apart without actually moving. The rubber in the balloon is stretching in much the same way that space is stretching.

Unfortunately, this analogy fails as one considers the fact that a balloon obviously expands into adjacent space. Or put another way, the volume of the balloon increases at the expense of the volume of its surroundings. The universe is not expanding into anything; it is just getting bigger. Of course, one could claim that there are extra-dimensional realities outside of our universe into which space is expanding. However this sort of thing has no physical reality as far as we are concerned. Therefore extra-dimensional realities are not capable of being studied scientifically. Any consideration of such things would be a philosophical exercise at best. The claim that the universe must expand into something hardly constitutes a flaw in cosmology.

THE BIG BANG DID NOT BEGIN AT ONE POINT IN SPACE OR IN TIME

A commonly held misconception is that while the big bang occurred at a finite time in the past, space and time are eternal. That is, space and time have always existed, and the big bang happened at some instant in time and some location in space. Most people visualize the big bang by first imagining that space was empty for a very long time before the big bang. They also pretend that if we had been present in the eternal empty space, we could have visualized that each of the three dimensions of space were number lines that intersected at one point. We could consider that point to be the origin of a three-dimensional Cartesian coordinate system. As we watched this very boring, empty universe for a long time, absolutely nothing happened. That is, until at some time the big bang suddenly appeared at the origin of the coordinate system. From its very hot, high-density beginning as a point, all of the matter and energy of the universe explosively expanded to fill space and eventually produced the universe that we see today, many of billions of years after the big bang.

While this is the common understanding of the big bang, it is completely wrong. First, according to the theory, the big bang was not an explosion of mass and energy into space in time, but rather it was an explosion of space and time as well. Not only did matter and energy come into existence at the big bang, but space and time did as well. There was no space before the big bang, but neither was there time. Sometimes people question the big bang by asking, "What was here before the big bang?" This is an improper question, because "here" was not here then. For that matter, "then" was not then

then either. This may seem contradictory or silly, but carefully consider the consequences of space and time commencing with the big bang. The concept of "here" requires that space exist. If space does not exist, then "here" cannot exist either. The words "then" and "before" depend upon the existence of time. If time does not exist, then the concepts of "then" and "before" have no meaning. So the very term "before the big bang" is meaningless.

Our mode of thinking is so linked to causality and sequential events that it is difficult to understand what is meant by this. This may seem illogical to the layman, but this is the current concept of the big bang. Unfortunately, many people who do have a grasp of the big-bang theory fail to see the consequences of no time prior to the big bang. We shall explore this in another section.

One result of space originating in the big bang is that the big bang did not occur at one point or one location of the universe and then spread elsewhere. Instead, the big bang happened everywhere in the universe. The difference was that the universe was quite a bit smaller back then. Thus it is incorrect to imagine that the big bang happened at some point or location and then spread elsewhere into space. Nor can one ask where the big bang happened, for it happened everywhere.

OLBER'S PARADOX HAS NO BEARING ON MODERN COSMOLOGY

In 1826, H. W. M. Olber developed an idea that squarely contradicted the cosmology of his time. Suppose that the universe is eternal and infinite and that stars uniformly inhabit it. In such a universe our view in every direction eventually would be blocked by stellar surfaces. The

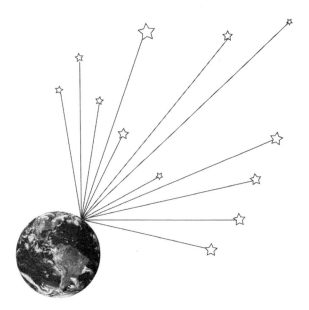

Olber's paradox states that our view in every direction eventually would be blocked by stellar surfaces

brightness of a star decreases by the inverse square of the distance, but the number of stars visible in this model increases with the square of the distance. These two factors exactly compensate, so that the sky in every direction should be as bright as a star, such as our sun. Therefore, the sky should be extremely bright, as bright as the sun. This expectation is in stark contrast to the observed darkness of the night sky. This has become known as Olber's paradox, though apparently others, such as Edmund Halley, discussed the matter a century before Olber.

Some creationists have used Olber's paradox to argue against the big bang and other evolutionary or atheistic cosmologies. However, how relevant is this objection? Let us examine the assumptions that lead to Olber's paradox and some of the suggested resolutions to the paradox. The first assumption is that the universe is infinite. Some attempted resolutions claim that general relativity does not allow for an infinite universe, but this is not true. The solutions to Einstein's equations allow for finite and infinite solutions, though many prefer the finite ones. The second assumption is that stars are uniformly distributed in the universe. That is obviously not true on any local scale, for stars are arranged in galaxies and galaxies tend to clump into clusters and super clusters. However, on a large scale this clumping appears less important. For comparison, we believe that the matter around us consists of many clumps called atoms, but for most purposes we can assume that objects are made of continuous distributions of mass. In the same fashion the universe may appear continuous on a grand scale. The third assumption is that the universe is eternal. With the big-bang model, the universe has a finite age, and this appears to be the best route for resolving Olber's paradox within the big-bang model. Before expounding on this, let us discuss some of the other suggested, but flawed, resolutions of Olber's paradox.

Within our galaxy and many other galaxies there is a huge amount of interstellar dust. This dust absorbs the light of more distant stars. Along the plane of the Milky Way the obscuration is so great that our view of distant stars is completely blocked. One suggestion is that interstellar dust absorbs so much of the light from stars that the night sky is dark. The problem with this resolution is that as the dust absorbs light, it is heated. In the infrared part of the spectrum we can see radiation due to the heat of this dust. With time, the dust temperature should increase so that eventually the dust ought to be nearly as bright as stars. Therefore, in an eternal universe this does not solve the problem.

Another suggested resolution is that redshift moves radiated energy from the visible into the infrared part of the spectrum, so that the amount of visible light is diminished. I was once taught this in an astronomy class. The problem with this is

that the redshift also moves energy normally in the ultraviolet into the visible. Therefore, as energy is moved out of the visible part of the spectrum, other energy takes its place. Thus this explanation fails to account for the dark sky as well.

As already mentioned, the key to resolving Olber's paradox is to examine the assumption of an eternal universe. In the time that Olber's paradox was discovered, scientists had long assumed that the universe was eternal. In the 20th century the acceptance of the big-bang theory convinced most scientists that the universe had a beginning and hence has a finite age. If the universe is, say, 15 billion years old, then we cannot receive light from anything more distant than 15 billion light years. It is as if we are located at the center of a spherical, finite universe that is 15 billion light years in radius. As far as the amount of light is concerned, it does not matter if the universe is finite or infinite, because we cannot see objects beyond 15 billion light years, a large, but finite distance. Given that the observable universe is finite, our view is not blocked by the surfaces of stars in every direction. In most directions we can see beyond all stars. Thus Olber's paradox is not a problem in a big-bang universe. The only relevance that Olber's paradox has today is in the context of an eternal universe, which is still supported by only a few adherents.

THE BIG BANG DOES NOT PROVE GOD'S EXISTENCE

As discussed in the introduction, since the time of the ancient Greeks until well into the 20th century many scientists assumed that the universe was eternal. One result of the big-bang theory is that it has convinced most scientists that the universe had a beginning. In a book written in 1978, the astronomer Robert Jastrow[2] pointed out that for the first time in history, mainstream science and the Bible agreed on the finite age of the universe. While Jastrow is an agnostic, he found it fascinating that modern science has begrudgingly come into agreement with the Bible on this one issue. Many contemporary Christian apologists go beyond Jastrow and argue that the big-bang model is in perfect agreement with the biblical account of creation, and furthermore that the big bang shows that God must exist.[3] There will not be a full discussion here of whether the big-bang model is compatible with the Bible. We will do that in the next chapter. Here we will explore the legitimacy of using the big bang to argue for God's existence.

The argument for God's existence using the big bang relies upon of the principle of causality. Causality means that any event that occurs (an effect) has some cause. Let A be a cause or agent that directly results in some event B. Then logically one can say that A causes B. A is the cause, and B is the effect. All effects in turn become causes of new effects, and so forth. At any time there are countless chains of cause and effect that are parallel and intertwined with one another. Conversely every effect must have a cause. Logicians and philosophers have long recognized that in the distant past there may have been an "uncaused cause." That is, there was a cause that was not the effect of an earlier cause, and from which all subsequent cause and effect relationships descended.

Of course many would identify the uncaused cause as God. However, in an eternal universe there would be no need of an uncaused cause, because cause and effect would have been operating over all time. This avoidance of an uncaused cause may have been the appeal that the eternal universe had in Western thought. As some Christian apologists point out, the big-bang theory posits that the universe had a beginning, so that an infinite chain of cause-and-effect relationships is no longer tenable. Jastrow would agree with this, but he would disagree on the identity of the uncaused cause. Christians would certainly identify the uncaused cause as the God of the Bible. Jastrow would insist that the big bang was the uncaused cause.

If A causes B, then B must occur after A does, for no effect can precede its cause. It is also doubtful that an effect and its cause can occur simultaneously. The approach of the Christian apologist is to argue that if B is the big bang, then the only cause, A, available is God, because nothing physical can precede the big bang. But this reveals a fundamental lack of understanding of the big-bang model, or causality, or both. Smith[4] makes this point in his discussion of the equations that give rise to the big bang. These equations relate physical qualities (space and time) of the universe. It is very clear that these equations suggest (or demand?) that time did not exist before the big bang. To ask a question such as "what was here before the big bang?" makes no sense, as discussed in an earlier section in this chapter. Time began with the big bang, and the big bang was the first event in time. Therefore the big bang had no antecedent. If time did not exist before the big bang, then any extrapolation of a temporal

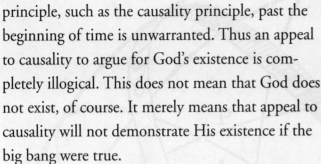

principle, such as the causality principle, past the beginning of time is unwarranted. Thus an appeal to causality to argue for God's existence is completely illogical. This does not mean that God does not exist, of course. It merely means that appeal to causality will not demonstrate His existence if the big bang were true.

Apologists generally attempt to sidestep this difficulty a couple of different ways. One way is to suggest that there is some extra-dimensional causality principle that works beyond our universe of which our causality principle bound by time is only a part. This is an appeal to a hypothetical principle that cannot be demonstrated, and hardly constitutes a good proof. Another approach is to argue for simultaneous cause and effect. If time began with the big bang, then an eternal God certainly would exist at the same time that the universe came into existence and thus could be shown to be the cause of the universe. The analogy is made to a soft cushion lying under a heavy weight, such as a bowling ball. The weight depresses the cushion, but can one say whether the weight causes the depression or whether the weight and the depression occur simultaneously? Physics clearly tells us that indeed the weight causes the depression in the pillow. That would seem to settle the matter as to what is the cause (the weight) and what is the effect (the depression). However some would respond that that is true in a finite situation, but would it be warranted in a situation where the weight and pillow were eternally existent? That question cannot be answered with confidence with either physics or logic. However to raise such an issue is grossly inconsistent with what is being argued. The entire point of the big bang-based apologetic is that the universe had a beginning. How then can one then invoke an eternal situation to support the line

of reasoning for God's existence using a non-eternal universe?

In summation, the use of the big bang to prove God's existence requires the use of the causality principle. However a cause must precede its effect. If the universe, via a big bang, is the effect, then its cause, God, must precede the big bang in time. The correct view of the big-bang model is one in which time began with the big bang. The big bang had no antecedent. Therefore the use of the causality argument across the boundary of time at the beginning of the universe is an unwarranted extrapolation. This does not argue against God's existence — it merely means that we can conclude nothing about His existence with this kind of argument.

As discussed in the previous chapter, much current research in cosmology is an attempt to explain how the universe could have come into existence in a fashion that is consistent with the physical laws that we observe within the universe. Since the universe had a beginning, there must be some uncaused cause. The theist will conclude that the uncaused cause is God. However the atheist or agnostic could just as well conclude that the big bang is the uncaused cause. Either conclusion appears to be valid. The atheist or agnostic could claim that his position has more validity, because the theist attempts to invoke two uncaused causes, the big bang and a deity.

Some Christian apologists today who accept the big-bang claim that the big-bang theory has caused many professionals in the field of cosmology to realize that there must be a Creator and thus have been led to the God of the Bible. This claim is misleading at best in that while there may be a few cosmologists and those who have written with some authority in cosmology who may have turned to Christ as a result of their studies, the vast majority have not. We have previously discussed the fact that Robert Jastrow (author of *God and the Astronomers*), while impressed with certain elements allegedly common to the Genesis and the big bang, remained an agnostic. In an interview Alan Guth was asked that if the universe could come from nothing (via his inflation model), what does that mean to us as human beings? Guth replied, "I think it undermines the belief that we are here for a any cosmic purpose. It does not mean that our lives are meaningless. It means we must give meaning to our lives ourselves." This is hardly consistent with a biblical world view.

Or consider the words of Steven Weinberg, author of the immensely popular book, *The First Three Minutes*[5]: "Ever since people started thinking systematically about the world, there's been a widespread impression that the universe exists partly to serve the interests of humanity. I don't think that's true…. The effort to understand the universe is one of the very few things that lifts human life a little above the level of farce and gives it some of the grace of tragedy." This, too, is antithetical to biblical Christianity or even to a personal God of any kind. In his very readable book, *Before the Beginning*,[6] Martin Rees does not raise the issue of God, but he does not have to, when one considers that his suggestion that we live in an immense "multiverse" containing an infinite number of universes is an attempt to explain how we and our apparently improbable big-bang universe could exist. It is obvious that in Rees's view there is no need for a Creator.

Perhaps some Christian apologists are confused by the fact that some cosmological researchers and writers even use the word "God" in some of their popular writings. For instance, Paul Davies has gone so far as to put God's name in the titles of two of his books dealing with cosmological questions (*God and the New Physics*[7] and *The Mind of God*[8]). Stephen Hawking uses the word "God" frequently in his best-selling book, *A Brief History of Time*.[9] However, anyone who carefully reads either of these two gentlemen will quickly find that neither one of them uses "God" to refer to anything remotely resembling the biblical God. Instead, they use God to mean an impersonal imposition of order (via natural law) upon the universe. Most researchers admit that they do not know how this order arises so that it does have a sort of mystical property, but suspect that the laws of nature probably reside in matter rather than space. There is a nearly universal hope that this mystery too shall fall with further work. In short, rather than being turned to the true and living God by their science, most modern cosmologists are engaging in a patently atheistic enterprise.

THE UNIVERSE DOES NOT HAVE TO HAVE A CENTER

The geometry that most people study is Euclidian geometry. Euclidian geometry is called this because its basic postulates were formulated by Euclid more than two millennia ago. Two-dimensional Euclidian geometry is sometimes called plane geometry, for the two dimensions lie in a plane. Also we could call plane geometry flat, because a plane is flat, meaning it has no curvature. In a plane, parallel lines do not intersect. Suppose that in a plane you have a line and a point not lying on that line. Then one, and only one, second line may be drawn through the point parallel to the first line. This is the fifth of Euclid's five postulates. This reasoning may be applied to a third dimension to produce solid Euclidian geometry. This, too, is a flat geometry.

Most people assume that the universe is flat, but is it? What is a non-flat, or non-Euclidian geometry? Go back to Euclid's fifth postulate. If that postulate is not true, then there are two possibilities. One possibility is that there are no parallel lines. The other possibility is that there is more than one line passing through a point parallel to another line. While both of these may seem strange, both are very real possibilities and have applications. The situation where there are no parallel lines is found on the surface of a sphere. It should be obvious that the surface of a sphere is not flat, so you should begin to see the difference between flat and curved geometries.

Many people think that the universe must have a center. If the universe is flat and finite, then it must have a center, but if the universe is infinite it will not have a center. However there are other possible geometries that may not require a center. The easiest example to consider is a finite universe that is curved back onto itself. Such a universe would have no boundary, or edge, yet one could travel indefinitely in one direction. A two dimensional analogue is the surface of the earth. Locally the earth's surface appears flat, because the radius of curvature is so large. One could travel forever in one direction, but of course that would require passing through one's starting point countless times. Does the earth's surface, or for that matter the surface of any sphere, have a center? Notice that I did not ask if the sphere had a center; I asked if the *surface* of the sphere has a center. Geometrically, the answer is of course no. In like fashion, if three-dimensional (spatial) space is finite and closes back

upon itself, then there can be no special point that we can call the center. In reality we do not know the nature of space enough to say if the universe has a center or not, though it is much easier to visualize a space that has no center.

THE CBR CANNOT BE CAUSED BY DUST OR STARLIGHT

As stated in chapter 1, the CBR is an impressive prediction of the big-bang model. The CBR is real, so one cannot deny its existence. Therefore if one wishes to replace the big-bang model, one must present a credible explanation for the CBR. Alternate explanations have been offered. Recent creationists and proponents of the steady-state theory have both proposed that dust is responsible for the CBR. The universe contains much dust, dust being microscopic solid particles. Dust particles may be made of various substances, such as silicates, ice, and iron. When exposed to starlight, dust particles will absorb energy and experience a temperature increase. Any object at a temperature above absolute zero (which is to say all objects) radiates energy. If an object has a temperature of 3K, then it will radiate with a blackbody curve having a peak in the microwave part of the spectrum very much like the CBR. Therefore uniformly distributed dust at a uniform temperature of 3K would produce the CBR.

However there are several problems with this explanation. First, dust is not uniformly distributed. In the Milky Way Galaxy dust is found very close to the galactic plane, and even within the galactic plane dust is very clumpy. In other spiral galaxies we see that dust is similarly distributed as in our galaxy. Given that dust is not homogeneously distributed, thermal radiation from dust should be very inhomogeneous, unlike the very smooth CBR. A second problem is that all dust clouds are at a much higher temperature than the CBR. Indeed, astronomers have found much emission from interstellar dust, but at a blackbody temperature much closer to 100K than 3K. In the far infrared part of the spectrum the galactic plane is very bright due to dust emission. One could counter that the CBR is the collected emission from dust in very distant sources and hence redshifted to the point that the observed temperature is much cooler than what was emitted. The problem with this solution is that galaxies are so clumped that we ought to see localized warm spots in the CBR due to large clusters of galaxies. As mentioned earlier, the CBR is so smooth as to be an embarrassment for the standard cosmology, but this solution fits the data even more poorly.

A similar appeal to greatly redshifted starlight as the source of the CBR is sometimes made. The reasoning is that the combined light of the many stars in countless galaxies at tremendous distances is blended together to appear homogeneous and is redshifted so much that the radiation corresponds to a 3K blackbody. The second argument against dust as the source of the CBR applies here as well. There is no evidence, despite its assumption, that the visible matter in the universe is homogeneous at any level. Even if there were homogeneity at some distant level, one would expect some foreground superclusters of galaxies to produce enough excess radiation to cause noticeable hot spots in the CBR. This is not seen.

THE COSMOLOGICAL CONSTANT IS NOT A FUDGE FACTOR

Sometimes the cosmological constant, Λ, is called a fudge factor. This stems from a misunderstanding of what Λ means physically and from a poor understanding of the history of the use of Λ. The history is that Einstein introduced Λ in his solution to the general relativity equation to produce a static universe. When we later discovered that the universe was expanding, Λ was revoked, but was more recently reintroduced to solve some potential problems with the standard model. Critics often ridicule the possibility of a non-zero Λ on the basis that it would act as some sort of anti-gravity, despite any experimental evidence of its existence.

If that were all that there was to it, the introduction of Λ would indeed be arbitrary. However, Einstein was quite justified in introducing Λ. The equations being solved are differential equations, a discipline that has wide application in many areas of science. The solution to any differential equation will have some constant of integration. The value of the constant is determined by the conditions placed upon the solution. The conditions are called boundary conditions, or, if the constant is determined by the values of some quantities at the start of the problem, they are called initial conditions. Often the constant of integration has zero value, but not always. The cosmological constant is such a quantity. Many think that Λ should be zero, but the possibility exists that it is not. Its value is determined by boundary conditions of the universe, but we do not know what those boundary conditions are. Every constant of integration has some physical meaning that is obvious from the nature of the problem. The meaning of Λ is that it is a repulsion term. Therefore Einstein solved the most general case (non-zero Λ), and then set Λ according to what he thought the boundary conditions of the universe were. This was a proper and legitimate thing to do, though it apparently was not the correct boundary value.

1. Are redshifts of galaxies due to the Doppler effect?

2. Can galaxies have a blueshift in an expanding universe?

3. What is the twin paradox? How is it resolved?

4. How can inflation cause things in the universe to separate faster than the speed of light, if things cannot travel faster than the speed of light?

5. Do redshifted galaxies appear red?

6. What does it mean that the speed of light is a constant?

7. Why is the "big bang" a bad name for the standard cosmological model?

8. What was here before the big bang?

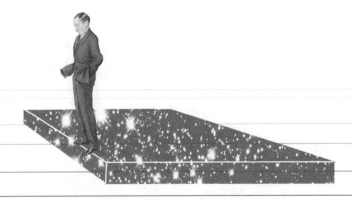

CHAPTER FOUR

PROBLEMS WITH THE BIG BANG

In chapter 2 we saw that three evidences for the big bang are usually given, the CBR, the expansion of the universe, and the abundances of the light elements. In that chapter it was argued that the first evidence is a clean prediction of the big bang, but that the last two are not, but instead are more aptly described as explanatory in nature. In this chapter we shall explore some of the difficulties that modern cosmology and the big bang have.

HALTON ARP

Since the late 1960s one of the more vocal critics of standard cosmology has been Halton "Chip" Arp. In two popular-level books,[1] Arp has laid out many of his objections. Much of his work concerns quasars. The first quasars were point radio sources identified in 1961. They appeared to be faint blue stars with a few unidentified emission lines. In 1963 Martin Schmidt showed that the spectral lines in one of these "radio stars" were hydrogen emission lines normally found in the UV part of the spectrum. To be seen in the visible part of the spectrum, the spectral lines would have to be shifted by 17%. This is a huge redshift, which meant that if the redshift was cosmological, the object had to be more than a billion light years away. The observed brightness meant that the radio star had to be far brighter than a typical bright galaxy.

At the same time, archival measurements of the brightness variations of the radio star over many years showed that the light irregularly varied over a time of only a few months. This was interpreted to mean that the object was at most only a few light months (the distance that light travels in a month) in size. This is required because any variation in brightness must be caused by some mechanism. There must be some "switch" that tells the material in the quasar to get brighter and then to get

Quasar

fainter. A signal must transmit this information. For a small object, such a signal can pass throughout the object virtually instantaneously. However, for a large object there will be some delay in transmitting this signal. The length of time for signal propagation, and hence the period of variability, is limited by the speed of the signal and the size of the object. The fastest known speed of propagation is the speed of light. If an object takes a month to vary in brightness, then it can be no more than a light month in size. This is an upper limit – the actual size is probably less.

Simply put, this radio star must be extremely bright and small. How can something be so small and yet so powerful? The new name, quasi-stellar object (QSO), was coined and that name was eventually contracted to "quasar."

Over the ensuing years many more quasars were discovered (there are now over 20,000 known), and naturally much more data has been collected. For instance, the first quasars were radio noisy, that is, they gave off much energy in the radio part of the spectrum. However, many quasars that give off little or no radio emission are now known. They are called radio quiet. Quasars have been found with various redshifts, but all quasar redshifts are very high.

Bridge

One of the best examples of galactical interaction is NGC 4319, which appears to have a luminous bridge between itself and Markarian 205.

Assuming that the Hubble relation is valid, their high redshifts suggest that quasars are at huge distances. Many quasars appear to have fuzzy glows around them, which astronomers think are the light of galaxies that host QSO's.

The picture that has emerged is that quasars are the cores of galaxies. Indeed, the cores of many galaxies without attendant quasars are found to exhibit quasar-like properties. A theory has been developed to explain how quasars can be so small and yet so powerful. We think that a quasar is a massive black hole containing millions of solar masses of material that is accreting matter from an orbiting disk. As the material descends into the steep gravitational potential well of the black hole, a huge amount of energy is released. Similar theories have been developed to explain somewhat less exotic goings on in galactic nuclei. In recent years observations made with the Hubble Space Telescope have revealed strong evidence

for massive black holes in nearby galaxies.

In summation, astronomers generally think that quasars are extremely distant, bright, small objects. The only theory we know that can explain the properties of quasars is that they are powered by super massive black holes. Arp has called this entire picture of quasars into question. He has suggested that quasar redshifts are not cosmological, and hence quasars are not that far away, and they are not that intrinsically bright. If this is true, then there is no great mystery about what is powering quasars. Arp is doing no less or more than doubting the principle that redshifts are cosmological. How has he done this? He has offered several lines of evidence, which we will now discuss.

Arp has taken photographs of several galaxies that appear to be interacting with other galaxies or with quasars. One of the best examples is NGC 4319, which appears to have a luminous bridge between itself and a nearby galaxy. Arp argues that the luminous bridge is material that is streaming from one galaxy to the other. To do so, the two galaxies must be at about the same distance from us. However, when the redshifts of the two galaxies are measured, they are very different, suggesting (via the Hubble relation) that the two galaxies lie at vastly different distances. If this is true, then the two galaxies cannot be interacting as suggested by the photographs. How have Arp's critics responded to this? They counter that the luminous bridge is an artifact or an illusion. The question really comes down to whether you believe what the redshifts tell us or if you believe what the images seem to tell us.

Arp has found other galaxies and/or quasars that show what appear to be arms of material from one object to the other. In some cases these arms are bent at peculiar angles that suggest a gravitational interaction between the objects. In every case the objects have radically different redshifts that would mean that the objects have very different distances if the redshifts are cosmological. Arp's critics respond that while these crooked arms of material are real, the objects in question are chance alignments. That is, the two objects appear to be interacting, because they lie in exactly the same direction, and one of the objects has a peculiar arm that appears to terminate on the other object. Arp counters by asking what is the probability for such chance alignments. These probabilities will be briefly discussed presently.

Another line of evidence that Arp has pursued is the alignment of quasars around nearby galaxies. He has found examples of nearby galaxies that have quasars clumped about them. If quasars are at fantastic distances, then they should be randomly distributed on the sky with some average density. In the cases where quasars are clumped around galaxies, the quasar density in the vicinity of the galaxies exceeds the average quasar density by orders of magnitude. Arp concludes that such density enhancements that just happen to line up with foreground galaxies are extremely unlikely. He thinks that it is more reasonable to conclude that the quasars in question are physically related to the galaxy around which they clump, and hence are not at huge distances.

It is one thing to critique the standard theory; it is another matter to replace that understanding with your own. In Arp's estimation, how are the quasars physically related to the host galaxies? He thinks that the quasars have been ejected from the galaxies. To support this contention, Arp has found examples of quasars that are not only clumped around a galaxy, but are along a line. In some cases this line coincides with a jet of material that is obviously shooting from the galaxy. Arp believes that quasars are ejected at high speeds from galaxies, but for some reason we only see the ones that are moving away from us. Perhaps any that are moving toward us (presumably half of them) are somehow obscured.

Arp's critics have responded that no matter how unlikely these alignments may seem, they happened and hence have a probability of 1. They

The Hubble image on the left, taken with the Wide Field Planetary Camera 2, shows the brilliant quasar but little else. The diffraction spikes demonstrate the quasar is truly a point-source of light (like a star) because the black hole's "central engine" is so compact. Once the blinding "headlight beam" of the quasar is blocked by the ACS (right), the host galaxy pops into view.

Quasar

Material jetting out

accuse Arp of improperly formulating the question. They say that he should have asked the probability before he found the data, rather than finding the data first and then asking the probability. This may seem like a picky point, but there is some validity to this criticism. Recall in chapter 2 we saw that the author of this book was quite improbable, but he happened. No one is amazed that he exists as he does, because he exists. For such a probability question to have meaning, the question should have been formulated before his conception.

Another example may illustrate this better. What is the probability that a fair coin when tossed will produce heads ten times in a row? It would be ½ to the tenth power. What is the probability that the tenth toss will be heads, given that the previous nine were all heads? Anyone who has studied probability theory will quickly realize that the probability is ½. The probability of a single toss is independent of any previous tosses. How and when one formulates the question is critical in calculating probabilities. No matter how improbable Arp's alignments may seem, Arp's critics insist that they happened, and so their probability is 1.

This line of reasoning confuses historical and scientific probabilities. Historical probabilities are either 1 or 0 — either something happened or it did not. In chapter 2, I used my existence as an example. My existence is not a scientific question; it is a historical question. I exist, so the probability of my existence is 1. We can

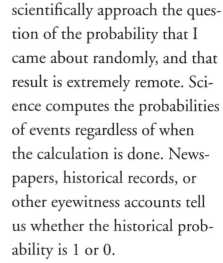

scientifically approach the question of the probability that I came about randomly, and that result is extremely remote. Science computes the probabilities of events regardless of when the calculation is done. Newspapers, historical records, or other eyewitness accounts tell us whether the historical probability is 1 or 0.

We use Arp's approach all of the time to rule out many explanations for phenomena on such grounds. In some criminal cases DNA evidence is used. DNA testing cannot uniquely identify a person as a fingerprint can. Instead, it merely tells us how well the DNA matches the suspect and the probability that it will match another randomly selected person. Suppose that in a particular case the DNA matches the suspect and that we are told that the match would be as good in only one instance in one million. In the estimation of most people, that would be pretty convincing evidence of guilt. However, if the city in which the crime occurred has three million people, the defense could argue that there likely are two other people who could have committed the crime. Of course the prosecution would resort to a probability argument, asking how likely it is that the suspect's and the true perpetrator's DNA match so well. Assuming the innocence of their client, the defense attorneys could claim that as unlikely as the scientific probability is, the historical probability is 1, because it happened.

As another example, consider a bucket of sand dumped upon a table. Each time that we dump the sand the individual sand grains end up in different locations. We could dump the sand onto the table a billion times, and the sand would never fall the same way twice. In other words, every dump would be equally improbable. Since the sand from each dump must end up in some arrangement, we are not amazed when the sand falls out a certain way. While the particular result of any single dump is highly improbable, each one happens in an historical sense, so the historical probability that it happened is 1. However, suppose that you entered a room where I told you that I had just dumped the sand onto a table. Upon inspection you notice that some of the sand grains make the outline of a few letters. As you read the letters you discover that they spell out the preamble to the United States Constitution. Of course you would not believe for a second that this was the result of a random dump of sand, and you would accuse me of arranging the sand this way. However I could counter that as unlikely as it seems; it did happen, so the probability is 1.

In the face of my defiant insistence that it happened, how could you pursue the probability argument? You would calculate the scientific probability that the sand arranged itself into those words by chance. You would find that the probability is so low as to be effectively 0. You would then know that in this historical instance, the probability is 1 that the sand was arranged by hand, not randomly dumped. The critics who object to Arp's probability argument are confusing scientific and historical probabilities.

Arp pursued his work with some of the largest telescopes in the world until 1986 when a group of influential astronomers who opposed him conspired to deny him any more telescope time. They made it clear that henceforth he could pursue more conventional research, but that his lifework was finished. Miffed at this outrageous action, Arp took an early retirement from California Institute of Technology and accepted a position in Germany. In the estimation of a minority of astronomers, Arp's work was never successfully refuted but was merely shouted down.

Arp has called into question the assumption of whether redshifts are cosmological — that is, if distance is related to redshift via the Hubble relation. If Arp is correct, then it is not so clear that the universe is expanding. If the universe is not expanding, then the big bang is not a viable theory, since that model was developed to explain the expansion. Arp does reject the big bang, though he apparently does not reject the expansion of the universe per se. Instead, Arp thinks that while redshift often reflects distance, it does not always do so. He believes that there are some large Doppler motions superimposed on the Hubble flow.

Arp's cosmology is a variant of the steady state. In the steady-state model, quasars cannot be distant. If quasars are all far away, then their great distances imply a look-back time. This means that we are looking at quasars not as they appear today, but as they appeared long ago. The fact that we do not see quasars nearby must mean that they no longer exist in the universe today. Therefore, the universe would look different at different times, which would violate the perfect cosmological principle, the basic assumption of the steady-state theory. This will be discussed in the next chapter.

We should restate an important point of Arp's work. If redshifts are not cosmological in many cases, then one must doubt if redshifts are cosmological in any case. If redshifts are not cosmological, then the universe is not expanding, and the big-bang theory is not possible.

QUANTIZED REDSHIFTS

Starting in the 1970s an astronomer named William Tifft discovered that galaxy redshifts are not uniformly and continuously distributed, but instead are quantized. In physics something is quantized if measurements of that thing's properties assume certain discrete values but not values in between. One of the foundations of quantum mechanics, the physics of small systems such as atoms, is that energy is quantized. That is, energy comes in small units and energy does not exist between those units. Tifft found that redshifts tend to occur in multiples of 72 km/sec. Later studies have found other multiples.

There is a bit of misconception on this point. Many erroneously think that the quantization is found in the redshifts as observed. This is not the case. The observed redshifts must be corrected for local motions. We have known for some time that the sun is orbiting in the Milky Way Galaxy at about 250 km/sec and that the Milky Way and local group of galaxies are moving as well. When these corrections are applied and a histogram of galaxy redshifts is plotted, the grouping of the redshifts at multiples of 72 km/sec is obvious. One difference between quantized redshifts and the quantization that occurs in quantum mechanic systems is that the quantization of quantum mechanical systems is absolute (there are no exceptions), while galaxy redshifts do have exceptions. That is, while quantum mechanical particles, such as electrons, are never observed to fall between two adjacent quanta, galaxy redshifts do frequently fall between the intervals of 72 km/sec.

What does the quantization of redshift mean to cosmology? It is not clear what it means. While most cosmologists doubt that

CBR picture of the Milky Way Galaxy

quantization is real, no one has been able to discredit it. Unlike Arp's work, this does not rely upon scientific probability arguments. Why are cosmologists so opposed to quantized redshifts? Primarily because they can find no reason for it, and the big-bang model cannot accommodate it. This whole topic is rather new and is due for more exploration. It could develop into a major problem for the big-bang theory.

On the other hand, a creation-based cosmological model that has been proposed has no problem with quantized redshifts. This model will be described in the next chapter. Just as quantized energy levels were fundamental to the establishment of quantum mechanics, perhaps quantized redshifts will be key in finding a new cosmology.

THE CBR

Earlier we saw that the CBR was a good prediction of the big-bang model. At the same time, properties of the CBR may be a problem for the big bang. The early universe must have been very smooth. Otherwise, any slight density enhancements would have acted as gravitational seeds to collect matter so that most of the matter in the universe would have long ago been sucked into black holes. On the other hand, if the universe had been exactly smooth, there would not have been any gravitational seeds to produce the structure that we see. The universe appears to be delicately balanced between these two extremes.

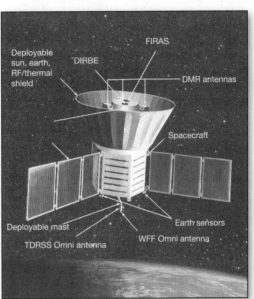

COBE satellite

Incidentally, this is another argument for the anthropic principle that has been developed.

The slight density enhancements in the early universe that allegedly allowed their gravity to collect matter into galaxies and other structures that we see today are called inhomogeneities. From the big-bang theory, cosmologists managed to calculate how much inhomogeneity the early universe ought to have had to produce the universe that we see today. This inhomogeneity should have left its imprint upon the CBR. During the 1980s a space probe named COBE was built to measure the calculated inhomogeneity. As the first data from COBE were assembled in the early 1990s, we found that the CBR was perfectly smooth. Only after two years of data were examined by a very powerful statistical method did the COBE researchers claim to have found the sought-after inhomogeneity. This was hailed as confirmation of the big-bang theory, but was it?

The COBE experiment was specifically designed to search for the expected inhomogeneity, but the experiment failed to find it as intended. That was because the inhomogeneity eventually claimed was an order of magnitude below what was predicted. How can the prediction be confirmed when it was off by an order of magnitude? In the wake of the discovery, big-bang models have been refined to account for the lower-than-expected inhomogeneity. What has been lost in most reporting of this is that the data did

83

not perfectly match the predictions, as is often claimed. This sort of reasoning has all-too-often happened with the big-bang model. A concordance of theory and measurement is proclaimed only after the data has been used to modify the model to "predict" the measurements.

A further question remains whether inhomogeneity has even been found. Only after very powerful statistical methods were applied to the data did anyone claim that the expected inhomogeneities had been found. No one could point to a particular direction in space and say that this was an area of higher- or lower-than-average temperature. Yet, most scientists were convinced that variations in temperature had indeed been found. Imagine if an astronomer showed you hundreds of stars in a dark sky and then proceeded to tell you that he has nearly 100% confidence that three of the stars are not stars but are actually planets. The only problem is, he cannot point to any individual star and tell you with complete assurance that it is actually a planet. Most people would consider such a proposition strange at best.

MISCELLANEOUS DIFFICULTIES WITH THE BIG BANG

The big-bang model has become so widely accepted that few have noticed the many nagging difficulties or have realized the numerous ways in which the model has been modified to handle some of these difficulties. Some of these have been discussed previously, but they should be mentioned here as well. The big bang depends upon the cosmological principle, but is the cosmological principle true? On the local level, galaxies obviously clump into clusters, but most cosmologists have assumed that on a grand scale

this clumping disappears. Extensive surveys of galaxy distributions have revealed that clumping and long strands of galaxies seem to be the norm on the largest scales that have been plumbed. The homogeneity of the universe is assumed, but all evidence indicates that the universe is not homogeneous. Or in other words, there is no evidence that the universe is indeed homogeneous. As for isotropy, the previously mentioned polarization study of distant radio sources indicates that there is some fundamental anisotropy in the universe. Therefore, there is considerable doubt that the cosmological principle upon which the big-bang model is based is true.

The COBE experiment was designed to measure the variations in the CBR that had been predicted by the standard big-bang model. COBE failed to detect the predicted variations, but studies of the data claimed to have found variations in the data at a level of an order of magnitude below those predicted by the model. Somehow this was hailed as a triumph of the big-bang theory. Few people seem to be aware that the big-bang theory was reengineered to fit the data. While discovery of variations in the CBR may be claimed as a qualitative victory, it certainly was a quantitative failure.

The horizon and flatness problems were described in a previous chapter. Inflation was created to explain these and other problems. Inflation is not universally accepted, it suffers from some difficulties of its own, and it amounts to speculation since little, if any, of it can be tested at this time. Most people who support the big bang would insist that inflation and recalculation of the big bang to fit the COBE data are merely refinements in the model. However, others legitimately view these as attempts to patch a flawed theory.

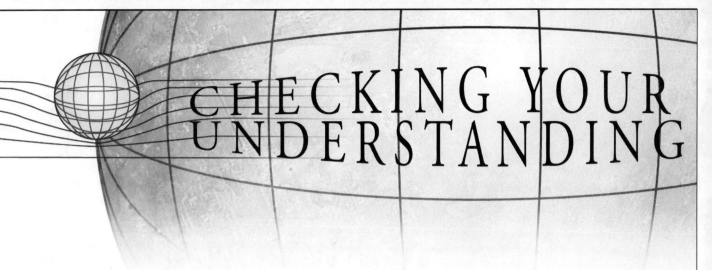
1. What do most astronomers think that quasars are?

2. What is the significance of Halton Arp's work?

3. What are quantized redshifts?

4. How well did the big bang predictions match the COBE observations?

5. Do we observe the universe to be homogeneous, as assumed by the big-bang theory?

CHAPTER FIVE

NON-BIBLICAL ALTERNATIVES TO THE BIG BANG

THE STEADY-STATE MODEL

The steady-state theory was briefly described in chapter 1, though the theory was not discussed much there. The reason is that most cosmologists (with a few notable exceptions) discarded the steady-state model during the 1960s because of the discovery of the CBR. There are other physical problems with the steady-state theory that we have not mentioned. These include the distributions of quasars and bright radio sources. Quasars are very rare locally, with none lying within a billion

Milky Way Galaxy

light years of the earth. At great distances quasars are quite common. It is very easy to show that the local density of quasars is much less than the quasar density at great distances. This violates the assumption that the universe is homogeneous, upon which both the steady-state and the big-bang theories are based. It also would seem to suggest that we lie at an unusual location in the universe, which violates the spirit of the Copernican revolution.

How can this be explained? In the big-bang model, when we look at distant objects we are looking at objects from a much earlier period in the universe. Greater distances correspond to greater look-back times. In a big-bang universe, the universe and the things in it change, or evolve, with time. So quasars must be objects that were common in the early universe but are now quite rare. However, in the steady-state model the universe as a whole does not evolve, though individual objects in the universe do so. At any given time there will be old and young objects mixed together. We would expect to see young objects such as quasars pretty much uniformly

scattered among old objects across the universe. In the steady-state theory we are also looking back into time when we look at distant objects, but the things that existed at that time would not be any different from the objects that exist today. So while the big-bang model can explain the sparseness of local quasars through evolution, the steady-state theory cannot appeal to evolution. Therefore, quasar statistics do not permit a homogeneous steady-state universe.

The statistics of bright radio sources are very similar to quasars (very few locally, but many at great distances), and so the same reasoning applies to them. In addition, astronomers have found that there are systematic changes in galaxies with distance. After correcting for redshift, distant galaxies appear bluer than nearby galaxies. Astronomers interpret this as evidence of intense star formation that must have happened early in the histories of galaxies. The steady-state theory posits that all galaxies are born and die and that in any particular location at any time one would expect to see a mixture of young and old galaxies. Even if the bluer colors of distant galaxies are not

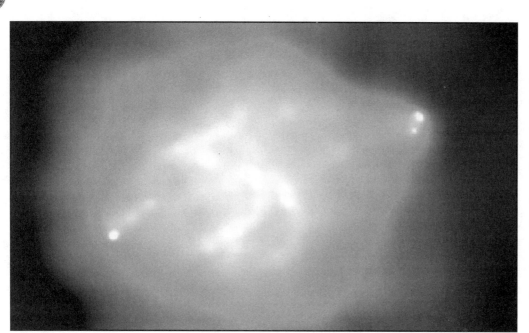

Recorded by the orbiting Chandra Observatory, Cygnus A is seen here as a spectacular high-energy x-ray source. But it is actually more famous at the low-energy end of the electromagnetic spectrum as one of the brightest celestial radio sources.

there would have been more-than-sufficient time for the universe to have reached a state of maximum entropy. This is obviously not the case. Steady-state theorists assume that as matter spontaneously appears to maintain a constant density, negative entropy is introduced to keep the entropy state of the universe at a constant as well.

due to evolution, the steady-state theory cannot explain this color difference.

In a big-bang universe, objects at great distances and in all directions would be systematically younger than nearby objects. This is true whether the universe has a center or not, because in either case all that is important is the distance from our location and how long it has taken light to travel to us.

A more basic problem with the steady-state theory is the second law of thermodynamics, the principle that energy, though conserved, is becoming less available for work. This increase in the lack of availability of energy is called entropy. The law of increasing entropy has been applied to information and complicated, well-working systems such as life. Many readers will recall its use in discussions of alleged biological evolution. It would seem that if the universe were eternal, as in the steady-state theory, then

According to the theory we do not notice either the addition of matter or negative entropy, because both are too small to observe on a local level. It should be emphasized that neither process has been observed; so one must question them on the basis of science.

This does not mean that the steady-state theory has been totally abandoned. The philosophical appeal of an eternal universe that requires no beginning (and hence no Creator) is quite strong. At one time many of the proponents of the steady-state model insisted that it had to be true, because it was so beautiful. The best example of a steady-state theorist is the late Sir Fred Hoyle. Hoyle continued work on a version of the steady-state model that would produce the CBR, but he did not succeed. All the while, Hoyle and others who support the steady-state theory have continued writing papers that are critical of the big-bang theory.

THE PLASMA UNIVERSE

Given that the steady-state theory enjoys very little support today, it does not warrant much discussion in a recent creation context. Therefore in this book we assume that the big bang is the only viable cosmological theory considered by most scientists. However, in recent years a new cosmology called the plasma universe has been proposed. The best source for this is the book by Eric Lerner.[1] One of the more noticeable adherents of this theory is the Nobel Prize winner, Hans Alfven. Plasma theorists point out that cosmologists generally assume that gravity is the only significant force that affects the structure of the universe, though gravity by far is the weakest of the fundamental forces. Electromagnetic forces are far stronger and are responsible for chemical bonds that cause most of the forces that we encounter every day. However, while the effect of gravity appears to have no limit over the distance that it operates, electromagnetic forces generally have a limited range. This limitation is due to the fact that most matter is electrically neutral.

Plasma theorists ask if this situation is necessarily true over all space. Is it possible that on a grand scale, electromagnetic forces may be as significant or greater than gravity? For instance, there may be some distance limitation on the pull of gravity about which we do not know. We do know that the galaxy is permeated by a

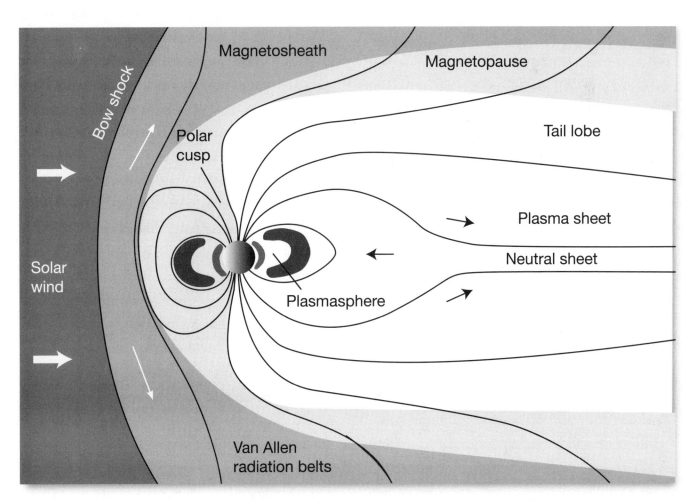

The Earth's magnetosphere

magnetic field, though its measured strength appears to be so small that its effects overall are far less than those of gravity. Plasma theorists also note that the spiral structure of galaxies is very similar to the pinch effect often produced in plasmas in laboratory experiments. Persistent spiral structure has been difficult to explain in terms of gravity alone, and so plasma theorists cite spiral structure as evidence that magnetic effects significantly affect matter on a large scale.

The plasma theory suggests that the universe is permeated with strong magnetic fields that confine how matter moves. If magnetic force dominates gravitational force over the large scale of the universe, then any cosmology that overlooks this is seriously flawed. In the plasma universe, magnetic force shapes local structure such as spiral galaxies and clusters of galaxies, but it also determines the structure of the universe as a whole. Plasma theorists believe that the universe is eternal and exists in a steady-state, but without the addition of mass as in the classical steady-state model.

How can this be reconciled with the observation that the universe is expanding? After all, if the universe is eternally expanding, there should have been more-than-ample time to have expanded the universe to virtually zero density. Plasma theorists reply that the universe has not always been expanding. Instead, there are regions of the universe that are now expanding, but there are others that are contracting. Expanding regions will eventually halt expansion and contract, while contracting regions will reverse and begin expanding at some time in the future. Different parts of the universe have been alternately expanding and contract-

ing in this fashion forever and will continue to do so forever. We just happen to live in a region of space that is expanding at this time. We also must be far from any neighboring regions that are contracting, or else we would see evidence of that. In other words, our expanding universe is merely a small subset of a much larger universe, and the extrapolation of the expansion back into time to a big bang is an unwarranted extrapolation.

There are a number of problems with the plasma cosmology. It asks us to accept some things that have not been observed. It cannot explain the CBR. The originators of the plasma universe have not explained how the increase in entropy with time can be circumvented. From a Christian perspective there are problems as well. The plasma cosmology is a return to an eternal universe, so there is no need or place for a Creator. While the big-bang cosmology has attracted a number of theists because it demands that the universe have a beginning, it is difficult to imagine that the plasma cosmology has any theists among its adherents.

The lack of alternatives to the big bang is testament to how pervasive belief in the big-bang theory has become. Since the 1960s very few scientists have thought it necessary to consider any other model. As during any scientific revolution, people hold onto the ruling paradigm long after numerous problems develop. Eventually some crucial results lead to the abandonment of the paradigm. After that there is some considerable casting about for an alternative. When the big bang falls into disfavor, one can expect that there will be no theoretical foundation for a substitute. At that time there will be many alternatives offered.

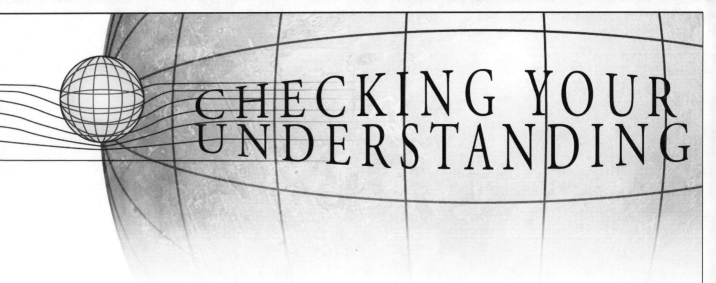

1. If quasar redshifts are cosmological, then all quasars are far away from us. Why is this a problem for

   the steady-state theory?

2. How can the big-bang theory explain why we do not see quasars locally?

3. How does the steady-state theory violate the second law of thermodynamics?

4. How is the plasma universe different from other cosmological models?

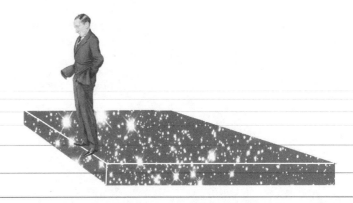

CHAPTER SIX

CREATION-BASED COSMOLOGIES

WHY THE BIG BANG IS NOT BIBLICAL

As discussed in chapters 1 and 3, there are many Christian theologians, scientists, and philosophers who accept the big-bang cosmology and make it part of their apologetics. The basis for this is that the big bang requires that the universe had a beginning, which was a clean break with belief in an eternal universe that had prevailed in western thought for a very long time. Many people think that the principle of causality necessitates that there must have been a cause, or Creator, of the universe. Therefore, many Christians think that the big bang proves that there is a God. As argued in chapter 3, people who think this fail to understand the big-bang model, the principle of causality, or both. Causality operates in time, so it is unwarranted to force its operation across a boundary of time such as the big bang.

Furthermore, as briefly discussed in chapter 2, there are theories being developed in cosmology that would have the universe come into existence in such a way that its beginning would not violate any physical laws. There are problems with these efforts, but they illustrate the philosophy and direction of those who have been the architects of the big-bang cosmology. Can these efforts be divorced from the big-bang model?

There is much danger in making a scientific or philosophical theory a very important part of our apologetic. There are some problems with the big bang, as discussed in chapter 4. The history of science tells us that most ideas that were once accepted as true were eventually abandoned in the light of later evidence. How many theories of a century ago are still believed today? It is very arrogant to believe that only our generation has found ultimate truth. An honest and humble examination of the history of science would tell us that there is an excellent chance that the big bang will not survive. If and when the big bang falls out of favor and we have made it a central theme of our apologetics, then what will happen to our apologetics?

There are biblical problems as well. It is no accident that nearly all Christians who embrace the big bang also accept a 4.6 billion-year-old earth. Belief in theistic evolution, or its stepchild, progressive creation, nearly always accompanies belief in an old earth. The first chapter of Genesis tells us that the creation was accomplished in six days, which would seem to contradict the vast periods of time that would be necessary for the big bang and an old earth. Nearly all who are old-uni-verse, old-earth creationists respond by appealing to the day-age theory, that the days of creation were vast periods of time. They point out that the Hebrew word for day, *yom*, can mean a period of time. That claim is true, but an important question is whether this is the intended meaning in Genesis chapter 1. There are compelling reasons that the days of the creation account are meant to be 24-hour days. The reasons for this have been discussed in detail elsewhere,[1] so only some of the reasons will be briefly addressed here.

On the first day of the creation week, light was created and was separated from darkness. God called the dark night and the light He called day. A verse later the text states that there was evening and morning of the first day. There are no verse divisions or punctuation in the Hebrew, but it is very clear from the context that all of the discussion of the first day represents a thought, perhaps equivalent to a paragraph in English. To use a single word with two very different meanings within a thought without clarifying which meaning is intended in either case would be very confusing and thus is sloppy writing. The first use of the word "day" is in the context of daylight and dark, and according to all rules of interpretation, grammar, and style, this is the definition that should be observed in what follows, but especially within that thought.

Each of the days of creation is preceded by an ordinal, or number (first day, second day, etc.). In ancient Hebrew when an ordinal is used with a day, it almost always refers to a 24-hour day. Some proponents of the day-age theory respond to this by pointing out that the only text of ancient Hebrew that we have is the Old Testament, and while that rule may be followed elsewhere in the Bible, is there any guarantee that that rule is indeed a rule of ancient Hebrew? That question can be answered several ways. One is to point out that Scripture must be interpreted with Scripture. If the rule concerning ordinals applies elsewhere, it should apply in the Creation account as well. Second, we do have examples of other ancient, non-Hebrew, Semitic texts, and they apparently follow this rule as well. Third, this is a rule generally followed in all languages. There is nothing mysterious about the Hebrew word *yom* — it has many of the nuances of our English word *day*. In English, if one numbers days, it is universally understood that 24-hour days are what is meant.

Exodus 20:11 states "For in six days the Lord made heaven and earth, the sea, and all that is in them, and rested on the seventh." This was written in the context of the command to observe the Sabbath. It is obvious that the Hebrews' workweek was six days. If the model that the Hebrews were to follow was the creation week, then it makes no sense that the days were long periods of time. The exegesis of day-age gets a little weird here, for it would lead to the nonsensical statement that first the Lord created in six time periods, and then much later He used this motif when giving the Law to the ancient Hebrews to hold His people to a very strict and literal

After the Creation of the Sun, Moon, and Planets by Michelangelo.

interpretation of the demands of a seven-day week, but the model upon which it was based is to be taken rather loosely.

This brings us to another objection to the day-age theory. When the modern version of the day-age theory began to be developed in the 19th century, it was hoped that the days of creation could be matched to geological ages. However, when one carefully compares the details of what modern science says about the history of the earth with the biblical creation account, one finds that there are marked differences. For instance, not only were plants created before the sun (the third day as opposed to the fourth day), but also the plants that are specifically mentioned are flowering plants, plants that according to evolution appeared very late, after the time of many of animals created on days 5 and 6. There are many other examples.

Given that the events of the six days of creation cannot be matched to the order of events that science professes, the original attempt to match creation days with geologic ages has utterly failed. However, the proponents of the day-age theory press onward anyway. How do these people propose to do this? Hugh Ross, one of the lead-ing proponents of the day-age theory today, has taught that the days of creation overlapped, so that creative acts of single days actually happened over several days. For example, Ross claims that dinosaurs, which as land creatures were created on day 6 according to Genesis, were created on day 5. How did Ross discover this? Unfortunately, not by studying the Bible, but instead by studying science and imposing his preconceptions and conclusion upon the Bible. In the absence of the pronouncements of modern science about origins, it is inconceivable that anyone would come up with such an understanding of the creation account. With such loose rules of interpretation, anything is possible. This sort of Bible exegesis would be viewed as heretical if applied elsewhere, but is ignored here because the alternative would not be palatable to so many.

Another approach to the creation account that is gaining ground in conservative circles is sometimes called the framework hypothesis.[2] Noting the subtle poetic aspects of the creation account, proponents of this idea argue that the creation account is primarily poetry. This theory is fraught with problems as well. First, this is a very new idea. With no real precedent in church history, one must question its legitimacy. As with the day-age theory, it is doubtful that anyone would think of this interpretation without the scientific pronouncements of origins. Another problem is the question of where does poetry end and the history begin? Were Noah and Abraham real people? Was the Tower of Babel a real event? If Noah was fictional but Abraham was real, where are the contextual reasons for such a claim? Most proponents of the framework hypothesis doubt the historicity of Adam and Noah. If this is true, then what are we to make of numerous New Testament references to both men, such as the words of Jesus in Matthew 24:38, Paul in 1 Corinthians 15, or Peter in 2 Peter 3?

The framework hypothesis overlooks the possibility that the creation account is history told with flair. It can be both poetry and history. Exodus 20:11 is even a larger problem with the framework hypothesis than with the day-age theory. If the six days of creation is merely a poetic device, then how could the Lord hold His people accountable to the very literal demands of the Sabbath and six-day workweek? If the model was poetry, could not the ancient Hebrews have interpreted at least this one commandment as poetry as well?

What all those who attempt to harmonize the big bang with Genesis miss is that the big bang is an evolutionary theory. In its basic form, evolution is an attempt to explain our existence and the existence of the world around us in a purely natural, purely physical process. This definition of evolution would apply to biological and geological evolution, as well as cosmic evolution. The big bang and biological evolution are cut from the same philosophical cloth. This is not a problem for the theistic evolutionist, but it should be. If one really understands what evolution is all about, then one will see that theism is wholly unnecessary. To bring God into the process as the Instigator is *ad hoc*. Unfortunately, many Christians mesh their apologetics with the atheistic enterprise of evolution in an attempt to gain favor with the scientific establishment. The sacrifice of biblical integrity in this attempt is sad.

Many Christian apologists today accept the big bang and claim that Genesis is in complete agreement with the big bang. However this is a situation driven by science and not by biblical studies. Prior to the widespread acceptance of the big bang during the 1960s many of those who peddled the idea that modern science and the Bible agreed so much on the question of origins rarely brought up a big-bang sort of origin for the universe. For example, the late Peter Stoner in a book[3] first published in 1958, is probably one of the best examples of this school of thought from the time period just prior to the near universal acceptance of the big bang. The name big bang does not appear in that book, though the basic elements of the big bang are briefly discussed. Very little detail is given about the origin of the universe, because much of the detail of the big-bang theory was yet to be developed. It would seem that if the agreement between the Bible and science were that good, then Bible scholars would have been able to guide the development of the big-bang theory. In reality it was the big bang that led to the development of this understanding of the Bible.

Therefore those who accept the big bang and make it part of their Christian apologetics are guilty of interpreting the Bible in terms of current science. This is a very dangerous precedent. However this sort of attitude is not new. For instance, the translators of the Greek Septuagint (LXX) rendered the Hebrew word *raqia* as *stereoma*, which Jerome followed as *firmamentum* in the Latin Vulgate, which in the AV (authorized, or King James Version) was transliterated as *firmament*. This is a terrible translation, and many modern translations break from this to render *raqia* as expanse. The word *stereoma* conveys the meaning of something hard, such as the crystalline spheres of ancient Greek cosmology upon which the stars were implanted.

Thus, the translators of the LXX incorporated the current cosmology of their day into their translation. This is very similar to those who wed the big bang to the Genesis creation account today. Other examples of reading current science into the Bible include secular chronologies of history that have caused some Christians to reinterpret biblical chronologies to fit. These attempts include a late date for the Exodus around 1200 B.C., about two centuries later than biblical chronologies will allow. Today there are other pressures bearing on biblical interpretations as well. Very questionable (but politically correct) studies have suggested that homosexuality is innate, that is, homosexuals have no choice in the matter. This does not square with the biblical injunctions against homosexuality. Unfortunately there are those who wish to reinterpret the Bible in the light of all new findings or latest fads of science, all the while claiming that this is what the Bible taught all along.

It is imperative that Bible-believing Christians take a right approach to the Bible and science. The Bible is either true or it is not. If it is true, then it is always true. On the other hand science is a very changeable thing. Most theories from a century ago have been replaced or heavily modified. It is very arrogant to think that only now have we really discovered the truth of physical reality. It is tempting to wed the Bible to our current understanding of the natural world, but that would be interpreting the perfect and unchangeable in light of the imperfect and changeable. Why would any Christian want to do that?

Simply put, the big-bang cosmogony is quite contrary to a very clear reading of the Genesis account. To distill the creation account down to the fact that the universe had a beginning, a fact

What we need is a biblically based cosmology and cosmogony. Thus far creationists have not spent much time building such a model, but have instead relied upon criticizing current cosmological and cosmogony models. If you will, this is big-bang bashing. Before discussing a few creation cosmology suggestions, let us describe some of this big-bang bashing. Some criticisms of the big bang are similar to the criticisms of secularists and atheists who also disagree with the big bang, though because of a very different philosophical basis.

that has only recently been confirmed by science, does great disservice to Genesis. We are given details of the creation week, and we ignore those details at our peril. The very clear teaching of the Genesis account is that the creation took six literal days. The big bang simply cannot be reconciled with this. The very strong implication is that the creation week was only a few thousand years ago. This seems scientifically embarrassing to many, so how do we prepare an effective apologetic within this constraint?

THE ORIGIN OF REDSHIFTS

Some people question the reality of redshifts. However, this is not a productive exercise. The redshifts are very real, though the interpretation certainly can be debated. Redshifts are usually understood to be radial Doppler shifts or due to the expansion of the universe, but could they be due to something else?

A number of alternate interpretations of the redshift have been offered. One is "tired light." Tired light is the theory that over distance light is somehow relieved of some of its energy, corresponding to a redshift. A mechanism of how this would happen has not been identified. Some have suggested that tired light is a result of entropy,

but there are questions about how and where the energy is transferred. Without a mechanism there are no predictions, so tired light cannot be tested. This removes this suggestion as a scientific idea and makes it more of a philosophical one. Tired light denies that the universe is expanding, but it does not address important cosmological issues such as the size, age, and history of the universe. Therefore it is not clear exactly what the purpose of the tired light proposal is, other than to deny the expansion of the universe. Some other cosmological statement or statements must accompany the tired light proposal.

West[4] has offered an alternate interpretation of the redshift as due to transverse Doppler shift. In this model the universe spins as a rigid body with the earth near the center. Nearby objects would move more slowly than more distant objects, but this motion is in the transverse direction, perpendicular to the line of sight so that it produces no classical Doppler shift. However, the little known transverse Doppler effect would be produced. This would result in Doppler shifts that are proportional to distance, much as what is observed. There are several problems with this however. One problem is, like the tired light theory, it offers no cosmological predictions nor does it offer a cosmogony. Another question is the nature of the rotation of the universe. Is the rotation one of matter with respect to space, or is it a rotation of space itself? If the rotation is one of matter in space, then distant objects would be moving far faster than the speed of light. If the rotation is of space itself (carrying matter along) then with respect to what is space rotating?

When all is said and done, these alternate explanations for redshift fall short. The simplest explanation of the redshift is that the universe is indeed expanding. Many of the questions concerning redshift appear to be subtle attacks on the big bang. If the universe is not expanding, then the big bang cannot be true. However, the big bang is only one possible explanation of the expansion of the universe. Are there creation-based alternatives? In rejecting universal expansion we could be throwing out an important datum that could guide development of a creationary cosmology.

THE LIGHT-TRAVEL-TIME PROBLEM

A thorny issue for recent creation is the light-travel-time problem. We will not take the time here to describe the various methods of finding astronomical distances. While there is some considerable error in these methods, they all result in very large distances, and even the most extreme errors possible will not decrease the overall distances by as much as a factor of two. These methods show that the universe is extremely large, many hundreds of millions, and even billions, of light years across. Presumably, it should have taken millions or billions of years for the light from these distant objects to reach the earth. If the creation was only a few thousand years ago, how

could the light from objects at such great distances have reached us? This is called the light-travel-time problem. Creationists have offered several resolutions of this problem. While these answers will not be fully described here, they will be briefly discussed with some of the advantages and disadvantages of each.

The most common response to the light-travel-time problem is to appeal to the concept of a mature creation. The trees in the Garden did not begin as seedlings, but instead were mature trees. The same was true of animals and of Adam. Undoubtedly each started out as a mature specimen; otherwise their functions would not have been met. In like fashion, the stars would not have fulfilled their purposes (provide light and to be for signs and mark seasons) if they had not been visible from the earth by day 6 (when Adam was created), and possibly as early as day 4 (when the stars were created). Therefore, perhaps light was created in transit already on its way toward earth so that stars were visible as early as day 4, but certainly by day 6 when man was created. Proponents of this answer claim that instant or rapid creation must be accompanied by an appearance of age. That is, a tree on the sixth day of creation would have appeared much the same as any mature tree does today. If we erroneously assume that trees can only come about through a long process of growth, then we will reach the incorrect conclusion that trees in the garden were many years old when in reality they were only three days old. This does not imply that we have been deceived, but rather that we have incorrectly assumed that there is only one way in which a tree can come about. In other words, we have not been fooled, but we have instead managed to fool ourselves. Thus things may appear mature to us only because we have made a uniformitarian assumption.

However, when this reasoning is applied to the universe, there are several differences. We all know what a mature tree looks like, but what does a mature universe look like? Indeed, many arguments for recent creation are that the universe looks young, but then we waffle by claiming that the universe has an appearance of age. If the universe appears young, then it should not appear old, and if it appears old, then we should not expect the

distant stars are an illusion. Since all galaxies outside of our own are much farther than a few thousand light years, we have never actually received light from any of these galaxies. Instead, light has been created as if it had come from these objects. If this is the case, must those objects actually exist? That is, if there is a created illusion, is there a need for the real objects?

Another problem is that the light from all astronomical objects contains very detailed information. From study of the spectra we can determine composition, temperature, motions, and a host of other things about astronomical bodies. For example, in 1987 a supernova was observed in the Large Magellanic Cloud, a small satellite galaxy of the Milky Way about 160,000 light years away. Astronomers were able to follow the rise and fall in the amount of light over many months. A hot, expanding gas cloud containing particular elements was seen. After a few years a light echo reflecting off nearby clouds was observed. All of this allowed astronomers to piece together

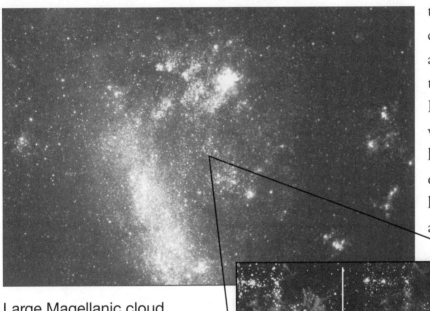

Large Magellanic cloud

1987 Supernova

universe to appear young. We cannot have it both ways.

With the mature-creation hypothesis, distant stars never emitted the light that we are now receiving from them. Instead, the light would have been created in transit and merely appear as if it had been emitted. There are two problems with this conclusion. One is the question of whether the stars exist at all. If starlight was created in transit and was never emitted by stars, then must stars exist? In other words, the creation of light in transit amounts to suggesting that at least the more

a pretty clear picture of the supernova event and its aftermath. However, the light created in transit theory would have us believe that none of these processes actually happened. Why would light created in transit contain so much information of physical processes that never happened?

Finally, the idea that light was created in transit makes no predictions, so it is not testable.

Therefore, it cannot be science. That does not mean that this idea is not true, but merely that it is more of a philosophical idea and not a scientific theory or hypothesis. Some critics have gone so far as to ask if most of the universe is an illusion, then why cannot all of the universe be an illusion? How do we know that the world was not created five minutes ago with memories of the past implanted in our brains? This, too, is philosophical and hence cannot be refuted scientifically.

A second explanation for the light-travel-time is a possible decrease in the speed of light. The Australian Barry Setterfield has pursued this idea. In the Setterfield[5] hypothesis the speed of light was much higher in the past, but has been exponentially decaying. Perhaps during the creation week the speed of light may have been nearly infinite. This would have allowed light from the most distant objects to have reached the earth during the creation week and continued to reach us as the speed of light has decayed over the years. Setterfield has attempted to relate the change in the speed of light to the fall or other events as well as to find other physical evidences. For instance, Setterfield believes that the decay in the speed of light can account for redshift without appealing to an expanding universe. To support his theory Setterfield has found measurements of the speed of light over the past three centuries that suggest that the speed of light has decreased and continues to decrease.

The Setterfield hypothesis is very controversial,[6] a subject that will not be fully discussed here. Critics of the Setterfield hypothesis usually make two points. One is that the speed of light is not an arbitrary constant that may be fixed at will, but is instead dependent upon physical parameters, the fine structure constant and the permittivity and permeability of free space. These two constants are very important in the behavior of electrons orbiting the nuclei of atoms. If those constants are changed even slightly, they will produce very noticeable changes in the structure of matter. If those constants are changed by even a fraction of the amount required by the huge change in the speed of light suggested by Setterfield, matter as we know it would have been impossible. Yet the spectra of distant objects appear identical to that of nearby objects, suggesting that the structure has not changed over time.

Another criticism of the Setterfield hypothesis is that the data may not support a decrease in the speed of light. The earliest measurements account for most of the change. Roemer made the first measurement of the speed of light over three centuries ago. This and subsequent early measurements indeed were much greater than those measured more recently. Taken at face value this would seem to indicate a decrease in the speed of light. However, the early measurements were subject to the greatest error, and it is entirely possible that Roemer simply determined a value that was too large. Those who measured the speed of light soon after Roemer may have fallen victim to trending. Trending is the tendency to make measurements close to the values already known. Science students do this sort of thing in laboratory exercises all the time. A savvy student will know what the book value of a measured quantity is, and the student will work toward this value as a guide. We would like to think that scientists are far too objective for trending to happen, but, being human, a scientist need not even be aware of such a bias. In fairness to Setterfield, he has found in the physics literature measurements of the speed of light made about a century ago by the famous experimental physicist, Albert Michelson. Michelson made several accurate measurements of the speed of light over several decades and apparently was convinced that there was a gradual change in the speed of light. This is much more convincing than the early measurements.

Another curious fact about the Setterfield hypothesis is that the speed of light has remained constant since the early 1960s. Setterfield has responded that new standards of time and length measurement adopted about that time are in terms of the speed of light. Therefore any measurement of the speed of light using the new standards will be in terms of the speed of light and must thus be constant.

A number of criticisms of the Setterfield hypothesis have been made. Some of these have been easily refuted while others have been more problematic. The Setterfield hypothesis remains a very controversial proposition among creationists, with scientists of good credentials and good arguments on either side. These sorts of disagreements are common in science and are a healthy thing. These and similar discussions should be encouraged. A final decision on this topic will not be soon in coming.

A BIBLICALLY BASED COSMOLOGY: THE HUMPHREYS MODEL

Russ Humphreys is a particle physicist who retired from a major research lab. From his knowledge of physics he knew that general relativity is one of the best-established theories of science. He was also aware of the light-travel-time problem. While contemplating this problem over several years, Humphreys was struck by Biblical mentions (as in Psalm 104:2) of the Lord stretching out the heavens. This seemed similar to the stretching or expanding of space as required by general relativity. Using this as a clue, Humphreys began studying general relativity with the intention of formulating a cosmology (or cosmogony) based upon the Genesis creation account that would solve the light-travel-time problem with relativistic effects. Humphreys has published an outline of his proposal in a book.[7] A full discussion of the Humphreys cosmology will not be attempted here; the reader is directed to the above reference for that. However a brief discussion of this model follows.

The Humphreys model assumes that general relativity is a reasonably correct theory of gravity and adequately describes the structure of the universe. One of the results of general relativity is that time is not an absolute for all space, but proceeds at different rates at different locations. The passage of time is affected by speed and acceleration, while those in turn are caused by the presence of large amounts of matter or energy. Time passes infinitesimally more quickly in the reduced gravity on a tall mountain, as compared to in a deep valley, but such small differences are extremely difficult to measure. If a large amount of mass or energy is present, the large curvature of space-time makes time pass at a slower rate than at a location where there is little mass or energy.

Humphreys's cosmology begins with the assumption that at the creation event of Genesis 1:1 all the matter in the universe was compacted into a sphere with a density equal to that of water. Amazingly, all of the matter in the universe would fit into a volume only about a light year across. We would expect that so much matter confined to such a small volume would be a black hole. Black holes are predicted by general relativity and

Black hole

are regions of space having such high density and gravity that nothing, not even light, can escape. A little-known fact is that a black hole is only one possible solution of such a configuration. Another equally valid solution is a white hole, so called for reasons that will be obvious in a moment.

A white hole is similar to a black hole, except that material is rushing outward rather than inward. The outrush of matter and energy would make a white hole appear very bright, unlike a dark black hole where no light can escape. A white hole is sort of the reverse of a black hole. When white holes were hypothesized during the 1960s, it became obvious that such objects could not exist today. One reason that white holes cannot exist today is that there is no natural way to produce such objects. On the other hand, astronomers have developed theories of how black holes can form. For example, we think that stellar-size black holes form from the catastrophic collapse of the cores of certain stars. Another reason that white

holes cannot exist today is that they are inherently unstable, so that any white holes from the beginning of the universe should have long ago ceased to exist. As matter streams out of a white hole, its diameter decreases. As the size approaches zero, the white hole disappears. Humphreys suggests that the universe began as a white hole that rapidly began to evaporate so that the white hole ceased to exist sometime during the creation week. Therefore the Humphreys cosmology is sometimes called the white hole cosmology.

Both black holes and white holes are bound by surfaces called event horizons. The event horizon conveniently divides space into those regions inside and outside the compact object. Just above the event-horizon time progresses much more slowly than it does farther away from it. Since the curvature of space is so extreme near the event horizon, the dilation, or slowing, of time is very pronounced there compared to regions far from the event horizon.

In the white hole cosmology, the earth is near the center of the universe so that it was among the last material to escape from the primordial white hole. Distant matter left much earlier. The creation account is told from the perspective of the earth, so the correct time frame is from there. On the earth the creation took six days. However, much of the universe may have left the white hole earlier than the earth and thus experienced much

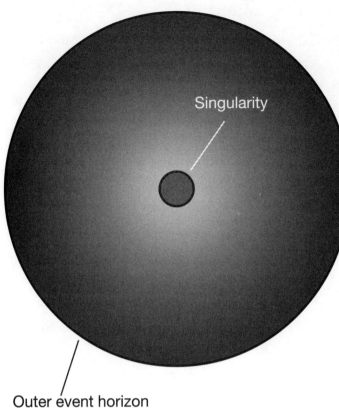

Singularity

Outer event horizon

greater lengths of time than six days. Because of the different rates of time involved, the stars could have been created on day 4, but the light would have traveled for many years to reach the earth within two days when man was here to see them.

Some may object that this is some sort of strange day-age theory, but it is not. General relativity tells us that time is not an absolute in this universe, but instead can run at very different rates. Indeed, general relativity demands that time pass at different rates at different locations in the universe. With certain initial conditions a literal day or two could have passed on the earth while permitting millions or even billions of years to have elapsed elsewhere. Such things are possible as a consequence of general relativity. Therefore the Humphreys cosmology could provide a resolution to the light-travel-time problem.

When introduced, the Humphreys white hole cosmology became quite popular, though not many people really understood how the model worked. Most creationists who are suspicious of the model have remained silent, mostly because it is difficult to credibly critique something about which you know very little. After a while a few old-age creationists began to raise objections to the white hole cosmology. Many of these objections have been minor problems or have been disagreements over how realistic some initial conditions that Humphreys assumed are. The white hole cosmology promises to be debated for some time.

We should emphasize that Humphreys actually proposed far less than many people think. Contrary to popular conception, Humphreys has not published a model, but rather he has suggested a very broad outline of what he wants the model to become. There are many details of the model that have yet to be worked out at the time of publication of this book. While preparing this manuscript I reviewed a paper by Humphreys submitted for publication. In that paper Humphreys discussed William Tifft's work on quantized redshifts. While redshift quantization is not explainable in terms of a big-bang model, it is easy to explain in Humphreys' cosmology. Taken at face value and assuming that redshifts are cosmological, the most likely conclusion is that we are located near the center of many concentric shells of galaxies. This means that the universe has a center and that we are located very near that center, which are clearly presuppositions of the Humphreys's cosmology. Of course, both of these ideas are anathema to any big-bang model so far proposed. This is promising. Whether or not the Humphreys cosmology survives, we should be encouraged by its proposal. Not only is it a serious attempt to solve the light-travel-time problem, but it also offers a biblically based cosmology, something that has been heretofore missing. I consider it likely that the solution to the light-travel-time problem is along these lines.

NON-EUCLIDEAN GEOMETRY

Before moving on we should discuss one other proposed resolution of the light-travel-time problem. In the 1950s two physicists named Moon and Spenser (not creationists) proposed that light travels through a different sort of (non-Euclidian) geometry than normal (Euclidean) space.[8] Euclidean space is flat, while non-Euclidean space is curved. One of the possibilities of modern cosmology is that space, while it appears flat, may be curved. This is not as weird as it seems at first. For instance, the surface of the earth is curved, but locally it appears flat. Apparently these two scientists proposed their model as an alternative to general relativity. They also stated their intention to follow their paper with subsequent work to clarify their model, but this never happened.

An interesting aspect of their model is that light from the most distant portions of the universe would arrive on the earth within 16 years. If such a model were true, it would be an obvious resolution of the light-travel-time problem. However, there are several problems. One is the question of how realistic this model is. They proposed that matter inhabits Euclidean space while light travels through a different kind of space. That is, the space that we inhabit is flat, but light travels through a highly curved space. Is there evidence

that this is indeed the case? One would expect that the promised future papers on the topic would have addressed this question, but, alas, that did not happen.

There may be one unintended prediction of the model. Moon and Spenser picked the radius of curvature of their model based upon a quirk. They realized that in their model very close binary stars would produce multiple images of the stars involved. This would cause unusual increases in the amount of light at various phases of the orbits. When Moon and Spenser published their work, few very close binary stars had been studied. Since that time many more close binary stars have been studied. Additionally, binary stars in which the companion stars are much closer together have been discovered. We now know of stars that are so close that it takes only a matter of minutes to orbit one another. Moon and Spenser selected a curvature small enough so that the effect of multiple images in the then-known binary stars would not be seen, but large enough so that its effects would not be observed in the solar system. With distant solar system probes such as the Pioneers 10 and 11 and the Voyagers 1 and 2 this limit has been increased as well. It is doubtful that using this data unavailable to Moon and Spenser would allow a refinement of their model that would work.

The light-travel-time problem still awaits a totally satisfactory resolution by recent creationists. Instead of majoring on this problem, perhaps we should realize that only an unbelievably powerful Creator could make such a large universe while at the same time enabling us to see it all. Instead of a problem, it could be one of the most remarkable testaments to God's creation.

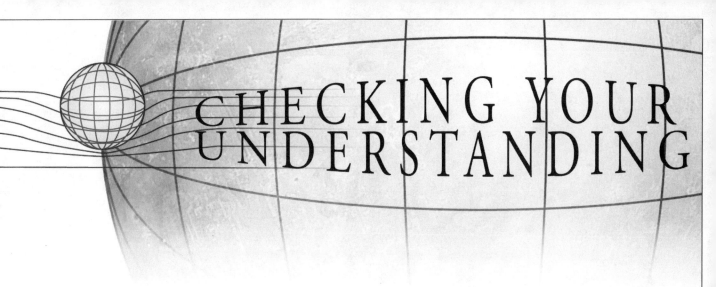

1. What is the day-age theory?

2. What is the framework hypothesis?

3. How does this chapter define evolution?

4. Why do some creationists reject the expansion of the universe, such as by appealing to the tired-light idea?

5. How is the translation of the Hebrew word *raqia* as *stereoma* in the Septuagint similar to people today who interpret Genesis to reflect the big bang?

6. What is the light-travel-time problem?

7. What is a white hole?

8. Why do most cosmologists doubt that white holes exist in the universe today?

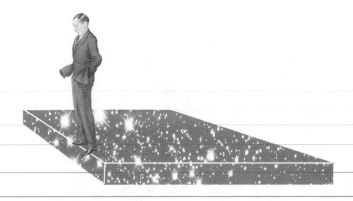

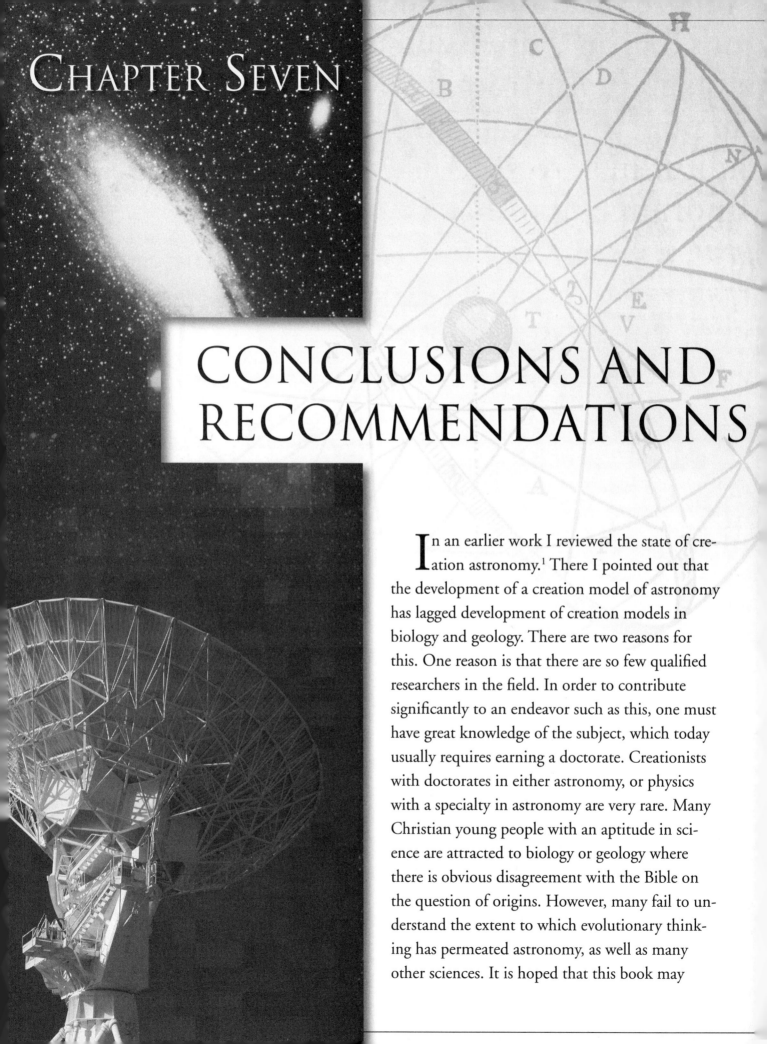

CHAPTER SEVEN

CONCLUSIONS AND RECOMMENDATIONS

In an earlier work I reviewed the state of creation astronomy.[1] There I pointed out that the development of a creation model of astronomy has lagged development of creation models in biology and geology. There are two reasons for this. One reason is that there are so few qualified researchers in the field. In order to contribute significantly to an endeavor such as this, one must have great knowledge of the subject, which today usually requires earning a doctorate. Creationists with doctorates in either astronomy, or physics with a specialty in astronomy are very rare. Many Christian young people with an aptitude in science are attracted to biology or geology where there is obvious disagreement with the Bible on the question of origins. However, many fail to understand the extent to which evolutionary thinking has permeated astronomy, as well as many other sciences. It is hoped that this book may kindle a keen interest and devotion in some Christian young people to pursue a career in astronomy to help develop creation-based models.

The second reason why so little progress has been made with a creation astronomy model is that we have fewer biblical specifics in astronomy as compared to biology and geology. Many of the issues dealing with biology and geology are post-creation week, while most astronomy issues may be creation week. Physics as now ordained to operate may have not been in effect at the time the astronomical world was created. The creation of the heavens is mentioned in Genesis 1:1, but it is unclear exactly what this means. The only other mention of astronomical bodies is on day 4 when the sun, moon, and stars were created. Does the creation of the heavens in Genesis 1:1 refer to the abode of God, or to space, or does it imply the creation of some material objects as well? Some would place the creation of distant astronomical objects at this time, but this would seem to contradict the very clear statement in Genesis 1:19 that those objects were created on day 4. Therefore, the creation of stars and galaxies in the very beginning (before the earth) is not biblically sound.

Alternately, the creation of the heavens on day 1 in Genesis 1:1 could refer to the initial creation of matter that on day 4 was shaped into stars and other objects. If all matter was created on day 1, then this raises the question of what form that matter was in. Was this matter merely amorphous, or did it have some shape? Was the matter "normal" matter, as we know it, such as atoms made of electrons, protons, and neutrons, or was it in some exotic form? All answers to these questions are speculative, as we have no firm biblical guidance on these issues. This situation does allow us some latitude in developing ideas. For example, in his model discussed in the previous chapter, Russ Humphreys assumes that the matter was normal atomic matter, primarily in the form of hydrogen and oxygen to form water. The speculation of water comes from the mention of water in Genesis 1:3 and water being placed above the expanse in Genesis 1:6-7.

With such scanty information, creationists generally have postulated that God created the astronomical world, probably entirely on the fourth day. This has been the extent of creation cosmology. This is contrasted with creation biology and geology. Creation biologists discuss baraminology, the study of created kinds, and question whether speciation within kinds has occurred since the Flood. Flood geologists offer evidence of catastrophic mechanisms that operated during and immediately after the Flood, and

Creation of the Animals by Jacopo Tintoretto

they use the Flood and its aftermath to explain the geologic column and the many varied landforms on the earth today. There are several competing theories of how the Flood commenced and laid down rock strata.

In short, creationists believe that events have shaped the earth and the life on it. Even the creation week may have contained some processes (albeit very rapid ones!) rather than instantaneous creation, though instantaneous creation may have been the norm. For instance, man was created from the dust of the earth, which suggested a shaping process. The fashioning of Eve from the side of Adam also suggests a process. The terminology of Genesis 1:11, 20, and 24 suggests that plants and animals may not have been created *ex nihilo*, but may have been created in a rapid process using matter that already existed. Each of these three verses says "let the earth (or water) bring forth. . . ." These words suggest the possibility of a process, however there are severe limits on any processes involved. The most severe limit would be that all creative processes would have

required less than a day, so these were not evolutionary processes.

Most creationists assume that bodies in the astronomical realm were instantaneously created on day 4, but is this necessarily true? Could these bodies have been shaped rapidly? Perhaps all the matter of the universe was created on day 1, but most of it remained shapeless until day 4, much as the earth was shapeless at first (Genesis 1:2). If this is true, then astronomical bodies may have been formed on the fourth day through a rapid, directed process. Again, because of its quick and ordered nature, this was not an evolutionary process. This suggestion catches the essence of the Humphreys cosmology. Matter was created in the beginning, but it was not until day 4 that stars and other astronomical bodies were formed. Perhaps the planets formed on the fourth day from matter created three days earlier. One possibility is that the many of the craters found on nearly every hard surface in the solar system were the result of the assembly of these bodies on day 4.[2]

What of the universe as a whole? The Humphreys cosmology is the only example of a serious attempt to explain how the universe came to be from a biblical framework. There may be other possibilities, but few people have spent enough time to develop them. It is desirable that we have a selection of cosmological models like we do with Flood geology.

In the Bible (Genesis chapter 1) the Hebrew word that is usually translated "heaven" is *shemayim*. A related word is the Hebrew word *raqia*, which was discussed in an earlier chapter. There it was pointed out that this was badly translated as "firmament" in the AV. Firmament gives the meaning of being hard, and was actually introduced in the LXX as an accommodation of ancient Greek cosmology. The word *raqia* is a noun that comes from a verb meaning "to beat out" as one might do to a metal. Gold is so malleable that gold working is a good example of this process. Hammers or rollers may be used to pound gold into a thin leaf that is only a few atoms thick. Gold leaf can be applied as a coating to surfaces in a process called gilding. Therefore, the *raqia* is something that is beaten out.

Obviously, the *raqia* must have some property of something that has been beaten out, but just what is that property? Some people who support the rendering "firmament" argue that the thing being beaten out is usually a metal, and since hardness is a common metallic property, the *raqia* must be something hard. However, there are other metallic properties, such as luster and electrical and thermal conductivity. Why should we restrict the meaning to hardness? Furthermore, gold is one of the best examples of a metal that is beaten out, but gold is not known for hardness. Perhaps the important property is not anything inherent in the thing beaten out but rather is a result of the process itself. When something is beaten out, it is stretched, so the *raqia* could be something that is stretched. This is especially interesting in that the Old Testament has numerous statements of the heavens being stretched out, as in Psalm 104:2. In fact, just these passages provided some inspiration to Russ

Humphreys for his model. If we understand the stretching of the heavens to mean the expansion of the universe, either past or present, then the Christian should welcome redshifts, not oppose them.

Many modern translations of the Bible follow this lead in rendering *raqia* as "expanse." In Genesis 1:14 the stars are said to be in the *raqia* of the *shamayim*, and in Genesis 1:20 birds are described as flying in the *raqia* of the *shamayim*. Thus a good alternate meaning may be the sky. In English we say that both birds and stars are in the sky. In other passages the heavens (*shamayim*) and the expanse (*raqia*) are equated. For instance, Genesis 1:8 explicitly states that God called the "*raqia*" *shamayim*. Therefore, the *shamayim* and the *raqia* may be used interchangeably. If this is correct, then there may be no basis for always making a distinction between the two — the two may be used as variety to mean the same thing or may refer to different aspects of the same thing. In any case, it is very clear that the *raqia* is not something hard.

Some people think that the creation of the *raqia* refers to the creation of space itself. If this is true, then what are we to make of the statement in Genesis 1:1 that God created the heavens (*shamayim*) at the very beginning? Others think that that the creation of the *raqia* on the fourth day refers to the creation of the earth's atmosphere. If this is true, then what are the waters above the *raqia*? Proponents of the canopy theory (that there was a large volume of water above the earth's atmosphere before the Flood) think that the *raqia* is the earth's atmosphere and that the water above was the canopy that was collapsed at the time of the Flood. Others think that this water refers to atmospheric water in the form of vapor and clouds. Still others think that there is a large amount of water beyond the space that we see in the universe. At least a few creationists think that the *raqia* is the creation of the crust of the earth or the earth's surface. This interpretation is difficult to square with some of the other considerations just discussed. We have no definite answers on just what is meant by these passages, and so some latitude in speculation on this is allowed. However, the best interpretation is that space itself was created in the first verse with the creation of the heavens.

One of the most serious shortcomings of creation astronomy is that there is no creation model of stellar astronomy. Again, most creationists conclude that stars were created on day four and have not changed since then. However, we assume that the earth changed dramatically during the Flood. We also believe that there may have been post-flood speciation and that many kinds of plants and animals have become extinct since the creation. Very little has been written on applying these sorts of principles to astronomy, so let us consider a few points here.

Our sun

Most astronomers think that over long periods of time, stars gradually change. This is based upon the conclusion that stars derive their energy from thermonuclear reactions, most notably the fusion of hydrogen into helium. Recent studies of solar neutrinos seem to confirm that at the very least the sun does this. Thermonuclear reactions generally happen in the cores of stars, where the pressure and temperature are high enough to

support these reactions. Thermonuclear energy is so efficient that stars could be powered over very long periods of time. For instance, calculation shows that the sun can be powered by this mechanism for about 10 billion years. Through fusion, the composition of the core of the sun and other stars should slowly change from being mostly hydrogen to being almost entirely helium. This change in composition will increase the mean molecular weight of the core. Anyone familiar with the ideal gas law will realize that as the mean molecular weight increases, there will be a change in the temperature and volume of the core. More specifically, the core will shrink and become hotter. The increase in the temperature and density will cause the thermonuclear reactions to increase. An increased thermonuclear reaction will cause the star to become brighter.

If a star changes its observable properties such as it brightness, astronomers say that the star has evolved. In other words, change is equated with evolution. Biologists try to get away with this sort of sleight of hand when discussing biological evolution. They define evolution as change, so if any change in the gene pool of a species can be demonstrated, then evolution can be demonstrated. Of course, most people recognize that biological evolution, if it were possible, is more than simple change. Biological evolution must include increased information and the development of new kinds of organisms. Astronomers do not claim that of either of these things happen with stars: stars may change their

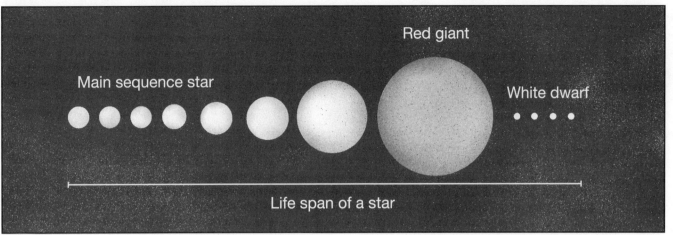

This illustration demonstrates the process of stellar aging.

properties, but no new information is generated and no new kinds of objects are created. This would seem to mean that stellar evolution and biological evolution are fundamentally different.

Another difference between stellar evolution and biological evolution is that the former is based upon well-established physical principles. Biological evolution would have to operate contrary to much of the same physics, such as the second law of thermodynamics. If stars derive their energy from thermonuclear reactions and if there has been sufficient time, then physics demands that stars must change their overall properties. That is, stars must evolve, given the definition of stellar evolution.

Many creationists are naturally taken aback by the possibility that stars can change, particularly when the word evolution is involved. Instead of saying that stars evolve, may I suggest the word "entrope"? This word is derived from the word entropy, for any changes in stars are subject to the second law of thermodynamics, and this word better reflects this fact than the word evolve does. Others have suggested the use of the alternate term "stellar aging," which gets across a similar idea.

The only impediment to observing stellar entroping is a lack of time. It takes a very long time for a star like the sun to undergo a significant change in its structure that can be seen. Indeed, if the universe is only a few thousand years old as the creation model suggests, then there has not been nearly enough time for most stars to have appreciably changed (or evolved, or entroped) from the state in which they were created. On the other hand, if the sun and earth were billions of years old, the gradual change in the sun demanded by stellar evolution theory is a problem.[3]

Through much of our discussion, we have assumed that the sun is a star. Developments in astronomy over the last few centuries have led us to this conclusion. However, is this true in a biblical sense? The Hebrew word for star refers to any bright, star-like object in the sky. Besides the stars, this term would include the planets, comets, and meteors. In short, virtually every astronomical body except the sun and the moon would be considered stars in ancient Hebrew. Even orbiting spacecraft visible to the eye and modern aircraft, especially at night, would fit the biblical definition of stars. In a biblical sense, the sun may not be a star. If this is true, then perhaps the sun is different from stars in some fundamental way(s). One possible avenue for creation research is to ascertain ways, if any, that the sun is different from stars. In passing, I should mention that some Christians note that stars are sometimes used in the Bible to represent angels, or messengers, and so conclude that distant stars are angelic beings. While interesting, this is poor theology and ultimately could lead to very strange beliefs. Nearly all, if not all, commentators agree that such usage is symbolic.

Many creationists believe that a major part of the curse as the result of man's sin in the Garden of Eden was the imposition of the second law of thermodynamics. The first law of thermodynamics insures that energy (and matter) cannot be created or destroyed, but the second law of thermodynamics is a statement of how less useful energy becomes as it is used. A quantity called entropy is the measure of how less useful energy is. The second law requires that entropy increase with time. Entropy has been generalized to not only refer to energy, but also to order and information, and to decay. Much of the case for the law of entropy being part of the curse is from Romans 8:22 and the context therein.

However, could this be reading too much into the curse? Digestion of food is an excellent example of the second law of thermodynamics. Food containing lower entropy is consumed to produce higher entropy waste, all the while producing energy and nutrients for the person eating. Did Adam and Eve eat before the fall? Certainly, given the instructions of what they could and could not eat and the fact that they sinned while eating. The second law of thermodynamics dictates the direction that energy flows (from hotter to colder). If the second law of thermodynamics did not work, then how could the sun and stars have shone before the fall? There are numerous other examples. This demonstrates that the second law of thermodynamics had to be in operation before the fall of mankind. If one wants to persist in arguing that the second law of thermodynamics came into force at the time of the fall, then one must hypothesize that some other law describing energy transfer was placed before the fall that the law of entropy supplanted at the time of the fall. While this is a logical possibility (one that I would not necessarily oppose), such a suggestion is hardly science, for it is not testable.

I bring this question up to ask just what effect did the fall of man have upon the cosmos? Romans 8:22 strongly indicates that the entire cosmos somehow shared in the curse. Any creation cosmological model should consider this and other questions raised here. At the time of this writing these questions have hardly been raised, let alone answered. It is my sincere hope and prayer that this modest book may help stimulate work on this important topic.

One thing that we have learned from our study of cosmology is that it is a rapidly changing thing. Over the years many ideas have seemingly been beyond dispute only later to be discarded. An understanding of Genesis that was tied to any of these ideas would have been discredited long ago. Are we so arrogant to think that only our generation has finally learned the ultimate nature of the universe? Those who would link Genesis to the big bang should carefully consider the caution offered here. When the big-bang theory is scrapped, what is to become of Genesis if we have wrapped it in the big-bang theory? Science is a tentative, changing enterprise, but the Bible is forever true.

1. Why has there been so little progress in developing a creation model of astronomy?

2. How might the Hebrew word, *raqia*, translated "firmament" in the AV relate to the modern idea of the expansion of the universe?

3. What is a star, as used in the biblical sense?

4. What does Romans 8:22 suggest about the universe and the curse of sin?

5. What is the danger of incorporating the big bang as the basis for understanding the Genesis account of creation?

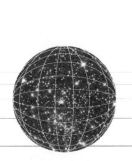

APPENDIX

OBSERVATIONAL ASTRONOMY: HOW WE KNOW WHAT WE KNOW ABOUT THE STARS

SPECTRA OF LIGHT

Almost all that we know about astronomical bodies we have learned by studying electromagnetic radiation. The most familiar kind of electromagnetic radiation is light. Light is a wave phenomenon, and as such possesses wavelength and frequency. The product of wavelength and frequency is the speed of light. Since the speed of light is a constant, an increase in wavelength corresponds to a decrease in frequency and vice versa. Red light has the longest wavelength visible to the human eye, and violet has the shortest wavelength that we can see. The middle of the visible spectrum has a yellow-green color and is the peak of sensitivity of the human eye.

At wavelengths just too short for the eye to see is the ultraviolet (UV) part of the spectrum. At even shorter wavelengths are x-rays and γ-rays (gamma rays). At the longer wavelength end of the spectrum beyond what we can see is infrared (IR). Beyond IR are microwaves and radio waves of various types. For instance, FM radio waves have higher frequencies and shorter wavelengths than AM radio waves. All of these waves are examples of electromagnetic radiation.

While the wave theory of electromagnetic radiation explains much, there is another theory that electromagnetic radiation is made of photons, tiny particles that have no mass. In this view, the energy of a photon is directly proportional to the frequency (or inversely proportional to the wavelength). Ultraviolet photons have enough energy to cause considerable damage to cells in our skin. Photons at higher frequencies contain even more energy. For example, the high energy of x-rays causes them to penetrate tissues, which makes x-rays an excellent medical diagnostic tool. Unfortunately this same high energy makes x-rays dangerous, because as the photons penetrate the body, cells can absorb their energy. The absorption of this energy results in damage to cell structures, especially DNA. This can lead to serious mutations that cause death or cancer. Therefore, much care must be exercised in the use of x-rays.

Many astronomical sources emit radiation in these harmful parts of the spectrum. Fortunately, the earth's atmosphere blocks nearly all of these dangerous rays and keeps them from reaching the ground. The earth's atmosphere also blocks much of the IR. This is just as well,

because the blocking goes both ways: IR radiation is kept in as well as kept out. The blocking of IR radiation is the greenhouse effect that keeps the earth's surface much warmer than it would be otherwise. While all this spectral blocking is helpful for life, it is most unfortunate for astronomy, because much information is carried in the portions of the spectrum that are blocked.

After World War II, technologies for exploring parts of the spectrum other than optical were developed. The radio part of the spectrum can be detected from the ground, but the radio portion remained untapped until after World War II. In the immediate post-war era many advances were made in radio astronomy. Additionally, astronomers began exploring parts of the spectrum not available from the ground with brief, high altitude flights with captured German V2 rockets. Later these sorts of experiments were continued with rockets developed in the United States and were supplemented by high altitude balloon flights. In recent years various orbiting observatories have greatly expanded our knowledge by allowing us to access the IR, UV, x-rays, and γ-rays.

Perhaps the best-known orbiting observatory is the Hubble Space Telescope (HST). The HST is able to observe the visible and near UV. While

most of these wavelengths can be studied from the ground, the HST was placed in orbit to avoid the blurring effects of the earth's atmosphere. As starlight passes through the atmosphere, changing densities due to temperature changes cause the light to follow slightly different paths. The rapidly changing light paths make stars twinkle. Twinkling leads to blurred images. Large telescopes can never realize their full image-making ability because of this blurring. Above the earth's atmosphere the HST has no problem with atmospheric blurring, so it has unparalleled resolution.

TELESCOPES

The heart of a telescope is its light-gathering device, which is called the objective. If the objective is a convex lens, the telescope is called a refractor, because the lens bends, or refracts, light to form an image. The other type of telescope is the reflector, so called because it uses a concave

mirror that reflects light to form the image. The important functions of the objective are to collect light and form an image. The size of a telescope is defined by the diameter of the objective. For instance, a 60 mm telescope has an objective that is 60 mm in diameter. The HST has an objective that is 2.4 meters. The largest optical telescopes are the twin 10-meter Keck telescopes at the Mauna Kea Observatory in Hawaii.

What are the advantages of a larger telescope? One advantage is that larger telescopes, having more objective surface area, gather more light. More light causes images to appear brighter. Distant objects too faint to be seen with a smaller telescope may be visible in larger telescopes. Since the observed brightness of an object decreases with distance, this means that larger telescopes allow us to study ever more distant objects. Another advantage of larger telescopes is that they produce more resolution. Resolution is the ability to see fine detail. This is especially

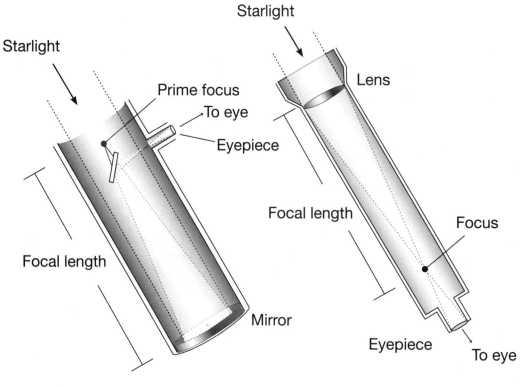

Reflector Telescope   Refractor Telescope

noticeable with the planets. A larger telescope usually will show features that will not be visible in smaller telescopes. However, the previously mentioned blurring effect of the earth's atmosphere limits this.

The distance between a telescope objective and the image of a far away object is called the focal length. We may examine the image formed by the objective by magnifying the image with an ocular, or eyepiece. The amount of magnification, or power, is determined by dividing the focal length of the objective by the focal length of the eyepiece. For example, an eyepiece with a 20 mm focal length used with a telescope with a 1,000 mm focal length will produce a magnification of 50 times. That is, objects viewed will appear 50 times larger. This is usually expressed as 50x.

The amount of magnification of a telescope is often over-emphasized in advertisements. As magnification is increased, the image does get larger, but the amount of the collected light is not increased. A larger image means that the available light is spread over a greater area so that the image appears much fainter than at lower power. In addition, any blurring caused by the earth's atmosphere or imperfections in the optics will be greatly magnified by high powers. Therefore there is a limit to how much one may usefully magnify an image. A good rule is that the maximum magnification on the best nights should be no more than about 50x for each inch of diameter of objective. For instance, the highest power that one should ever use with a ten-inch telescope would be 500x. That would be the limit on the very best nights; on most nights less magnification should be used.

Professional astronomers spend little time peering through an eyepiece. Instead, equipment is attached to the telescope to measure and record the light. Sometimes the telescope is used as a camera lens to record an image. Once this was done with photographic emulsions, but the Charge Coupled Device (CCD) has largely replaced photography. A CCD is a computer chip with many small light sensitive elements that acquire charges proportional to the amount of light that falls upon them. To produce an image, a computer periodically reads the charges from the CCD. A CCD collects light much more efficiently than regular photographs can. Therefore, CCDs are much faster than photography, so that a one-minute CCD image can record as much light as a one-hour photograph. The studies of images can reveal much about celestial objects.

PHOTOMETRY

Besides direct imaging there are two other primary uses of telescopes. One is photometry. The word photometry comes from two words that mean "light measure," so photometry is the science of measuring light brightness. Many stars vary in brightness. Variable stars can change brightness for a number of reasons.

Measurements of star brightness give us the raw data that permits us to determine why a particular star varies in brightness.

Astronomers use magnitudes to express star brightness. This system was developed by the Greek astronomer Hipparchus two millennia ago. There are two peculiarities with the magnitude system. One is that the smaller numbers correspond to the brighter stars, while the higher numbers correspond to the fainter stars. The brightest stars in our sky are first magnitude, while the faintest visible to the unaided eye on a dark night are about sixth magnitude. The faintest objects detectable today are fainter than magnitude 30. The full moon is about -12.5 magnitude and the sun is -26.8. The other peculiarity is that the scale is logarithmic. The system is arranged so that each difference of one magnitude corresponds to a factor of about 2.5 in brightness. A difference of five magnitudes is defined to be a factor of exactly 100 in brightness.

As an example, consider a first magnitude and a sixth magnitude star. First magnitude stars are roughly the brightest stars in our sky, while sixth magnitude is the limit of what the naked eye can see on a clear, dark night. A sixth magnitude star is five magnitudes fainter than a first magnitude star. Therefore the sixth magnitude star is 100 times fainter. How many times fainter than a first magnitude star is an eleventh magnitude star? This is a difference of ten magnitudes. Since this is a difference of five magnitudes twice, some might erroneously conclude that the stars differ in brightness by 100 + 100 = 200. However, each magnitude difference of five is a multiplicative factor of 100. Therefore a ten-magnitude difference is a factor of 100 x 100 = 10,000 = 10^4. Similarly a fifteen-magnitude difference is a factor of 1,000,000 = 10^6.

What we have described thus far is apparent magnitude, how bright a star appears to us. However, a star's brightness depends upon two factors: how bright it actually is, and how far away the star is. In professional circles stellar distances are usually expressed in parsecs, a unit that will be described later. Most people are more familiar with light years; a parsec contains 3.26 light years. If a star's distance and apparent magnitude are known, then we can express the star's actual brightness as an absolute magnitude. Absolute magnitude is defined as the apparent magnitude that a star would have if it were 10 parsecs, or 32.6 light years, away. The sun has an absolute magnitude of 4.8. Let m be the apparent magnitude, M the absolute magnitude, and d be the distance expressed in parsecs. The these quantities are related through the equation

$$d = 10^{(m - M + 5)/5}.$$

Spectroscopy

A third use of a telescope is spectroscopy. A prism or diffraction grating disperses light, which means that the light is broken up into a spectrum of different wavelengths. A device attached to a telescope that does this is called a spectrograph, and a record of a spectrum is called a spectrogram. Studying stellar spectra can tell us much information about stars. These include things such as temperature, size, composition, and motion.

The simplest atom is that of hydrogen, which has a single electron orbiting the nucleus that

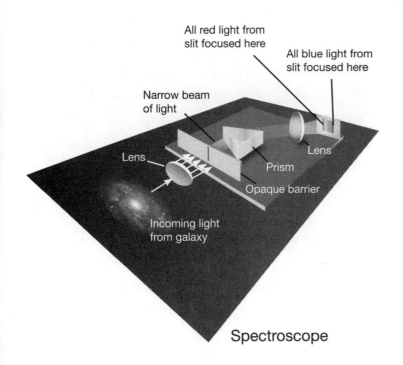

All red light from
slit focused here

All blue light from
slit focused here

Narrow beam
of light

Lens

Lens

Prism

Opaque barrier

Incoming light
from galaxy

Spectroscope

two orbits. Each orbit corresponds to some energy, with the innermost orbits having the least energy and the outermost having the most energy. Since the orbits are quantized, the energy of the electron is quantized as well. An electron can make a leap, or transition, from one orbit to another orbit. As an electron makes an upward transition from a lower to a higher orbit, it must gain energy. As an electron makes a downward transition from a higher to a lower state it must shed energy. One way that an electron can gain or lose energy is by the absorption or emission of a photon. Earlier in our discussion we found that the energy of a photon is directly proportional to the frequency of the photon. The greater the energy difference between two orbits, the greater the frequency of the photon involved.

usually contains one proton. Below is an illustration of a hydrogen atom. Notice that the electron can be found in one of a number of orbits. Each orbit is distinguished by a number designated as n, with n having positive integer values starting with one. The lowest orbit closest to the nucleus is designated n = 1, the next highest is designated n = 2, and so forth. As n increases in value, the orbits get closer together. For large values of the number n the orbits cram together toward a limiting maximum orbit size corresponding to a value of n approaching infinity. This limit of the orbit size amounts to the maximum size of the hydrogen atom.

Electron orbits are quantized. This means that electrons can be found only in orbits corresponding to an integer value of n as shown in the figure. An electron may not orbit part way between

Hydrogen atom

EMISSION SPECTRA

Suppose that an electron in a hydrogen atom is in the n = 3 orbit. The electron can make the downward transition to either the n = 1 or n = 2 state. Since these downward transitions emit a photon rather than absorb one, these transitions happen quite easily. Another way of looking at this is to realize that the electron is going from a higher energy state to a level of less energy. This is the natural direction of processes, as dictated by the second law of thermodynamics. Often the electron will make the transition from the n = 3 to the n = 2 state, with the emission of a photon having an energy equal to the energy difference between the second and third orbits. The energy of this photon corresponds to a frequency in the red part of the spectrum. This transition and the resulting red photon are called H.

Suppose that instead of starting in the n = 3 state, the electron started from the n = 4 state. The electron would then have the choices of falling to the n = 1, 2, or 3 state. Suppose that the electron again went to the n = 2 state. Since the n = 4 orbit has more initial energy than the n = 3 state, the emitted photon must have more energy than the H photon. The greater energy results in a higher frequency, and the color of this emitted photon is more toward the blue end of the spectrum than the H. Actually, it does appear blue. This emission is called H.

Now suppose that the electron was initially in the next higher state of n = 5. If the electron made the transition to the n = 2 state as before, the energy difference would be greater still and the frequency of the emitted photon would be even greater. This photon is in the violet portion of the spectrum, and is called H. This series can continue indefinitely with ever-higher initial orbits with successive Greek letters. The energy differences become less and less with higher terms, so that the frequencies of the photons get closer together. This series is called the Balmer series, after the German physicist by that name who discovered it experimentally in the latter part of the 19th century.

The Balmer series was an important bit of information that guided Neils Bohr to devise his model of the atom around 1914. This model, while a little naive, is the basic model of the atom that we have today, and is the version of the modern theory that most of us are taught in school. There are additional series resulting from other transitions in the hydrogen atom. For instance, the Lyman series is in the UV and results from transitions to the n = 1 state from higher levels. The Paschen series is the result of transitions between the n = 3 level and higher states, but it is in the IR. All of these other series lie outside of the visible part of the spectrum, so only the Balmer series may be readily observed by humans. Indeed, even in the Balmer series only the first three emission lines are visible. All subsequent lines beyond H lie in the UV beyond what the eye can see, though they may be photographed.

How do electrons get into the higher energy states to begin with? Electrons can be elevated to the higher orbits by inputting energy, such as by heating or electrical discharge. Electrical discharge is used in low-pressure lamps. Examples of low-pressure lamps include many streetlights and fluorescent lights. As the electrons fall to lower energy states they emit photons only at discrete energies as just described. Therefore the spectrum emitted will be dark except at those wavelengths where emission occurs. Such a spectrum is called a bright-line, or emission, spectrum because the spectrum will have bright emission lines in it. Hydrogen produces a geometric progression of three spectral lines at the frequencies (or alternately, wavelengths) in the visible part of the spectrum as just described.

In like fashion other elements produce sets of spectral lines. However, since the energy differences between states are not the same, the photon wavelengths and patterns are different. The result is that every element has a unique set of lines. This is the basis of chemical analysis using spectroscopy. If a sample is heated or excited to fluorescence, a spectrogram of the emission will show the lines of the elements present. Emission spectra result from hot gases at low pressure. Emission lines as just described are seen in the spectra of nebulae and the chromosphere, an upper layer in the sun's atmosphere.

ABSORPTION SPECTRA

Most stellar spectra are very different from emission spectra. A hot solid, liquid, or gas at high pressure produces continuous spectra, where all wavelengths or colors are seen without any lines. If the light from a continuous source passes through a cooler, low-pressure gas, an absorption spectrum is seen. Absorption spectra have bright backgrounds interrupted by dark absorption lines. Another name for an absorption spectrum is a dark-line spectrum. The interiors of stars are hot, high-pressure gases, so they produce continuous spectra. The outermost layers of stars (the stars' atmospheres) are cooler and less dense than the interior, so the resultant stellar spectra have absorption lines.

How do absorption lines form? The process is the reverse of that with emission lines. The electrons are initially in a lower state. If a photon having the correct amount of energy passes by, the electron can absorb the photon and use the photon's energy to make the transition to a higher orbit. Eventually the electron will emit another photon and fall back to a lower state, but the new photon will generally have a random direction so that there is a net loss of photons in the original direction of motion of the light (outward from the star's interior). For instance, electrons in hydrogen atoms initially in the $n = 2$ state can absorb photons having sufficient energy to elevate the electrons to the $n = 3$, 4, or 5 states.

The amount of energy absorbed in each of these transitions is the same as when emission occurs. Therefore the wavelengths (or frequencies) of the photons involved will be identical to those as seen in emission. Thus an absorption spectrum is like a negative of an emission spectrum. Other elements have absorption lines at the same wavelengths as their emission lines as well. The spectra of nearly all stars are absorption spectra. A few strange stars, called Wolf-Rayet stars, have emission spectra instead.

When the spectra of various stars are compared, it is obvious that there is a bewildering array of different spectral lines in different stars. To make sense of this mess, about a century ago Harvard College Observatory began a program of classifying stellar spectra. The system that eventually emerged was one based upon temperature. In order of decreasing temperature, the spectral types are O, B, A, F, G, K, and M. Each class is subdivided into 10 subclasses that run from 0 to 9. The sun has spectral type G2. A slightly hotter star would be a G1 subclass, while a slightly cooler one would be G3.

Stars of spectral type A have the most intense Balmer lines of hydrogen, while O and M types lack Balmer lines. In G-type stars like the sun, the Balmer lines are moderately weak. One might expect that the presence or absence of the spectral lines of a particular element would signal the presence or absence of the element itself, but this is not the case. The weakness of Balmer lines of hydrogen does not mean that hydrogen is uncommon in the sun or that the absence of Balmer lines in O and M type stars means that those stars lack hydrogen. In fact, hydrogen is believed to be the most common element in nearly all stars. For spectral lines of a particular element to be visible, the element obviously must be present, but the electrons must be in the correct initial orbits as well. In absorption the Balmer lines require that electrons initially be in the n = 2 state. At low temperatures most electrons will be in the ground, or n = 1, state. Therefore, if the temperature of a star is too cool, most of the electrons will be in the lowest state and thus will be unable to make a transition that will produce a Balmer photon. If a star is too hot, nearly all of the electrons will be in highly excited orbits or even ionized. Therefore there will be too few electrons in the n = 2 orbit to produce Balmer lines. In summation, hydrogen Balmer lines can exist in stars only having a certain temperature range. The peak of the Balmer lines, where the largest percentage of hydrogen atoms have their electrons in the n = 2 state, is at a temperature of about 10,000°K. This temperature corresponds to the A0 spectral type.

Other elements have similar constraints on their visibility. The hottest stars (spectral type O) have atmospheric temperatures of about 40,000°K, and the only lines in their spectra are due to ionized helium. Less hot stars have neutral helium lines and weak hydrogen lines. At cooler temperatures the hydrogen lines strengthen while the helium lines fade. The hydrogen lines reach a maximum in the A type. Progressing to cooler types, the hydrogen lines gradually fade and are replaced by ionized metal lines. By the time the coolest stars are reached (spectral type M with temperatures of about 3,000°K), neutral metal lines and bands due to some molecules are present. In conclusion, the basic spectral types are a function of temperature, not composition.

However, there are a few stars (less than 1%) that do have odd compositions that render their spectra very different from the vast majority of stars. A striking example is the group of stars called carbon stars. As the name suggests, carbon stars contain much carbon. Typically stars have more oxygen than carbon, but carbon is more abundant in carbon stars. In normal red-giant stars all of the carbon is used up in forming carbon monoxide (CO), leaving the oxygen to combine with metals to form metal oxides that dominate their spectra. In carbon stars all of the oxygen is used up, leaving the carbon to form various carbon compounds. These compounds and free metals in the atmospheres of carbon stars change the atmospheric structure of carbon stars. This makes them very different from normal red giants. One obvious difference is that carbon stars are often far redder than normal red-giant stars. Carbon stars have been classified as R or N types that parallel the K and M types in temperature. A more modern classification combines the R and N types into a single C class.

Related to carbon stars are the metal stars, classed as S type. Metal stars have odd metal abundances. For instance, some S stars contain the element technetium, of which there are no stable isotopes. There are other examples of stars with odd spectra, but usually they can be grouped with more "normal" spectral types with various appended letters to indicate their peculiarities. For instance, some stars are appended with an "e" to indicate emission or an "m" to indicate magnetic fields. Astronomers have developed evolutionary theories to explain how these odd stars became this way.

Temperatures can be determined by spectral type, but there are other ways, as well. One method is by measuring color. Color is a result of a difference in magnitude measured at different wavelengths. Astronomers have devised filters that allow us to measure different parts of the spectrum. Two of the most common are the B filter that is in the blue part of the spectrum and the V filter that is in the visual (yellow-green) part of the spectrum. Except for their absorption lines, the spectra of stars greatly resemble the spectra of blackbodies. A blackbody is an object that perfectly absorbs and radiates electromagnetic energy. They are called blackbodies because at lower temperatures, such as room temperature, they appear black. Obviously at high temperatures they appear bright.

The illustration below shows a comparison of the spectra of two blackbodies having different temperatures. Notice that the curve of the hotter temperature is higher than that of the cooler temperature. Also notice that the peak of the hotter curve is at a shorter wavelength than that of the cooler curve. To the eye, a hot star appears blue, while a cool star appears red. Intermediate temperature stars appear yellow, with various shades in between. The B filter is so situated that it is near the wavelength where the spectrum of a hot

star peaks, while the V filter is far from the peak. Therefore if magnitudes measured in either filter are compared, the B magnitude will be much brighter. However, for a cooler star the peak is nearer the V filter, and the B filter will be far from the peak. Therefore the V magnitude of a cooler star will be greater than the B magnitude. Since the magnitudes of a single star are what are being compared, the overall height of the curve is immaterial.

The magnitude difference is called a color index and is usually expressed as B-V. A very hot star might have a B-V of –0.10, while a very cool star might have a B-V of +1.70. The former star would appear blue and the latter would appear red. The sun is a yellow appearing, medium temperature star with a temperature a little less than 6,000°K. The B-V of the sun is about +0.62. This system of color index has been calibrated with accurate spectral types and generally offers a very efficient way to measure stellar temperatures.

STELLAR VELOCITY

Spectroscopic data can tell us how fast stars are moving toward or away from us by the Doppler shift. As discussed in chapter 3, Doppler shift and cosmological redshift are not the same thing, though they appear the same. If a star is moving away from us, the lines in its spectrum will be shifted to longer wavelengths, while a star moving toward us will have its lines shifted toward

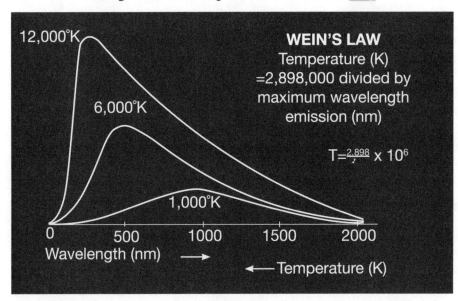

WEIN'S LAW
Temperature (K) = 2,898,000 divided by maximum wavelength emission (nm)

$$T = \frac{2.898}{\lambda} \times 10^6$$

As a blackbody heats, the wavelength of maximum emission shortens and energy radiated increases at all wavelengths.

shorter wavelengths. Many spectrographs can produce a laboratory spectrum of some material that can be recorded along with stellar spectra. We can calibrate the stellar spectra by comparing the laboratory and stellar spectra. Even small spectral shifts caused by motion of only a few kilometers per second can be measured this way. The only motions that spectroscopy can measure are those in the line of sight; transverse motion perpendicular to the line of sight cannot be measured this way. Line-of-sight motion is called radial velocity, while transverse motion is called tangential velocity.

Radial velocities are very helpful. For one thing, it is a direct confirmation that the earth moves around the sun. Our orbit around the sun causes the radial velocity of most stars to shift in a sinusoidal fashion throughout the year. That is, stars lying near the earth's orbit around the sun have their radial motions vary by plus and minus 30 km/sec each year. That speed is the rate at which the earth orbits the sun. Therefore radial velocity measurements must be corrected for this effect to express radial velocities with respect to the solar system. Since the sun is the center of the solar system, measured radial velocities corrected for the earth's motion around the sun are called heliocentric radial velocities. Heliocentric radial velocities tell us which stars are moving toward the sun and which are moving away, though the measured radial velocity is actually a combination of a star's motion and the motion of the sun. Analysis of radial velocities of a huge number of stars has enabled astronomers to determine what is called the local standard of rest. We also know that the sun is moving around the center of the galaxy at a speed of about 250 km/sec. This information allows us to estimate the mass of the galaxy.

Radial velocity measurements are very important in the study of binary stars. A binary star is a system of two stars that are orbiting around each other by their mutual gravity. As the members of a binary star orbit each other, they may alternately move toward and away from us, resulting in periodic Doppler shifts in the spectral lines. These shifts allow us to model the system and determine basic stellar parameters, such as mass. Close binary stars are the sites of many interesting astronomical phenomena. For instance, many close binary stars have mass transfer from one star to the other, a process that is readily observable with spectroscopy.

In recent years these kinds of radial velocities have been used to search for extra-solar planets, that is, planets orbiting other stars.[1] In a binary-star system, both stars move because either star pulls on the other with its gravity. Newton's third law of motion ensures that the amount of force on either is equal in magnitude. How much either star moves depends upon how similar their masses are. If the masses are equal, then the stars will move equally. If one star has more mass than the other, then the less massive star will move more, with the ratios of the stars' motions inversely proportional to the masses of the stars. In fact, this relationship is what allows us to determine the masses of stars in binary-star systems. Planets also move the sun, but because the sun has so much more mass than the planets, the planets do almost all of the moving while the sun does very little. The search for extra-solar planets relies upon looking for very subtle Doppler shifts in the candidate stars. A small periodic shift in a star's spectrum could be evidence of a planet orbiting that star. When one calculates the amount of mass required to produce these subtle orbital motions in a star and finds that the mass is far too small to be a star, then we are left with the conclusion that the unseen orbiting body must be a planet. Most astronomers agree that we have found many extra-solar planets, with the list growing.

The observation of extra-solar planets is not without controversy. Even single stars may exhibit periodic radial velocities. Many variable stars are pulsating. That is, they regularly expand and contract. As these stars expand and contract they alternately produce radial velocities toward and away from us that are superimposed upon their regular motion. As these stars expand and contract, their temperatures also change. You should recall that as a gas expands it cools, and as it is compressed it heats. The complex interplay of changing size and temperature causes pulsating stars to noticeably change in bright-

ness. This is what makes them variable stars. The very subtle periodic Doppler shifts in the candidate hosts of extra-solar planets are orders of magnitude lower than those of pulsating stars. Therefore some astronomers at first suggest that if the stars that allegedly host other planets are actually pulsating, then the small changes in the sizes of these stars might not be readily visible as light changes. This objection has been overcome to the satisfaction of most, and so this does not seem to be a way of explaining away the existence of extra-solar planets.

As an aside, is the existence of other planets a problem for the biblical world view? Not really. Most creationists assume (rightly so, I believe) that there is no life on other planets (extraterrestrial life). Some creationists apparently think that denying that there are other planets will somehow limit this possibility. However,

Artist's concept of a binary star system

we should welcome other planets. All of the planets discovered at the time of the writing of this book are obviously hostile to any form of life, because most are too massive or too close to their parent stars, or both. This should be a powerful witness to us that our planet is special. Even if some of these planets might be hospitable to life, we know that life from non-living matter apart from creation is impossible.

Tangential velocities are much more difficult to measure than radial velocities. Motion in the tangential direction results in a gradual change of a star's position in the sky. Comparison of photographs of stars made many years apart tell us how fast stars are changing position. The average annual change in position of a star is called the star's proper motion and is expressed in arc seconds per year. Most proper motions are very small. The largest proper motion is that of Barnard's Star which is only 11.2"/yr. Barnard's Star takes about 160 years to move the equivalent diameter of the moon. Proper motion depends both upon the tangential velocity and the distance. A star that is moving very rapidly in the tangential direction must not have a large proper motion if it is far away. Conversely, a star that is nearby may have a large proper motion but a modest tangential velocity. In order to find the tangential velocity, we must know both the proper motion and the distance. Generally the nearer stars have the larger, and hence more accurately known, proper motions. We also know the distances of nearby stars better. Therefore the measurement of tangential velocities is restricted to the nearer stars, while radial velocities may be found for any distance.

STELLAR MASS

The masses of stars are found by the study of binary stars. As stated above, the members of binary-star systems orbit by their mutual gravity. For a given separation, the orbital speed and period depend upon how much gravity is present. The amount of gravity in turn depends upon the amount of mass. The masses of hundreds of stars have been determined this way. The least massive stars are about 8% that of the sun, and the most massive are a few tens of times the mass of the sun. While we can find the masses of stars only in binary systems, we find in binary systems a wide range of stars that appear otherwise identical to solitary stars. Therefore it is reasonable to conclude that we know the masses of stars with confidence.

Astronomers have measured the mass of the galaxy by treating the sun and the galaxy as a binary-star system. As mentioned above, the sun is orbiting the galaxy with a speed of about 250 km/sec. We think that the sun is about 25,000 light years from the center. It is simple physics to calculate the acceleration and hence the mass necessary to keep the sun in orbit. The amount of mass is about 10^{11} solar masses. Similar studies of other objects orbiting our galaxy and other galaxies have indicated that dark matter may exist.

STELLAR SIZE

Eclipsing binary stars offer us a direct way of measuring the diameters of stars. An eclipsing binary is a binary in which the orbital plane is viewed nearly edge-on so that with every orbit the stars pass in front of, or eclipse, each other. Obviously, larger stars take longer to eclipse each other than smaller ones do, so the duration of the eclipses tell us how large the stars are. Perhaps hundreds of stars have had their sizes measured this way. When similar stars from different eclipsing binaries are compared, their sizes agree pretty well. This gives us confidence that when we see other stars that are not in eclipsing binary systems, but are otherwise similar to ones that are, then we probably know the sizes of those stars as well.

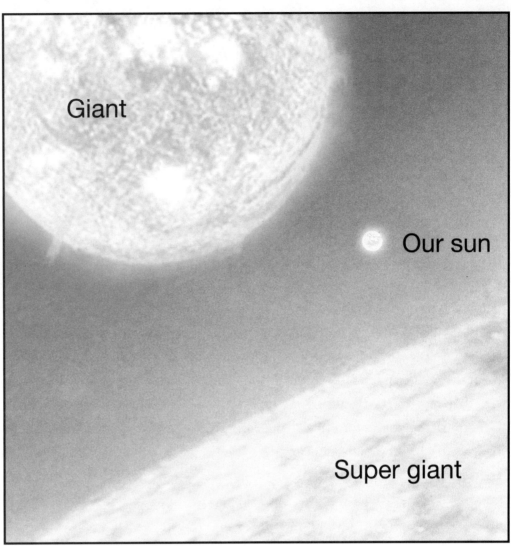

This illustration shows the difference in the size of our sun compared to the largest stars.

There are several indirect ways of finding the sizes of stars. From time to time the moon passes in front of a star, which is an event called an occultation. Both the star's disappearance behind the moon and its later reappearance on the other side happen very quickly (usually far less than a second). High-speed photometric measurements reveal that the star does not disappear instantaneously, but "gradually" over a tiny fraction of a second. Often this takes thousandths of a second. The rate at which the star disappears and later reappears depends upon several things such as the speed of the moon in its orbit,

the angle that the edge of the moon makes with the moon's motion, and the apparent size of the star. The apparent size is the angle subtended by the star, and is usually expressed in units of milli arc seconds, or thousands of a second of arc. All other factors are known, so from the data we can calculate how large the angular diameter is. However, we can convert the angular diameter to actual linear diameter (in kilometers) only if we know the distance to the star. This is why this is an indirect method. If the distance is not known, then the star's diameter cannot be found.

While the lunar occultation method works very well, the moon occults stars only found in a swath about 11 degrees wide centered along the ecliptic. Most stars are not found in this narrow region of the sky. Interferometry was discussed briefly in chapter 1. It is the technique of using the principle of interference resulting from the wave nature of light to glean certain information from the light. This can be done with the light of some stars to measure their angular diameters. As with the lunar occultation method, the distance of the star must be known to find the actual diameter, so this too is an indirect method. It also suffers from the limitation that only stars with very large angular diameters can be measured, so it is restricted to much larger angular diameter stars than the lunar occultation method.

A fourth method of finding stellar diameters involves using some well-understood physics. The Stefan-Boltzmann law states that the amount of energy given off by a blackbody goes at the fourth power of the temperature. In equation form,

$$L = \sigma T^4$$

where L is the luminosity (the total energy radiated per second), T is the temperature in Kelvin, and σ is a physical constant. The total brightness of a star also depends upon the surface area of the star. Stars are generally spherical, so the area should be $4\pi R^2$. These two equations can be combined into a single equation, but the units will be a bit cumbersome. Therefore, astronomers usually change to solar units to simplify the equation:

$$L = R^2 T^4$$

where L, R, and T are the luminosity, radius, andtemperature of a star expressed in solar units. What are solar units? They are the quantities in terms of the sun's units. For instance, the sun's luminosity is 3.88 x 10³³ erg/sec, so that amount is defined to be one. The sun's radius is 6.96 x 10¹⁰ cm, so that is the unit of radii. The sun's surface temperature is 5,770°K, so that is one unit of temperature.

This equation can be turned around to solve for R, but first we must know T and L. The determination of temperature is straightforward by spectral type of color as previously discussed. Luminosity is more difficult. We must know the distance to convert the apparent magnitude to absolute magnitude. Inverting an earlier equation that related these quantities can do this. However, both apparent and absolute magnitudes are measured at certain wavelengths, such as in the B or V filters. The luminosity must be expressed as the power released by a star when all wavelengths are considered. Such a magnitude is called the absolute bolometric magnitude. It is not possible to measure bolometric magnitudes, so we calculate them using what measurements we can and stitching together the rest of the spectrum and well-understood physics. Some astronomers have spent much of their professional careers preparing tables for other astronomers to make these transformations. Once an absolute bolometric magnitude has been found, we can easily convert this to luminosity to put in the equation.

Since this method of finding stellar sizes is not limited to stars along the ecliptic, it is very powerful. However, since it requires knowing the distance of each star measured, it is an indirect method. It is also dependent upon certain models, such as stellar-atmospheric models that permit the conversion of an observed magnitude into luminosity. This introduces error, but there are limits on that error. It is probable that we can determine sizes of stars by this method to within 20%.

FINDING STELLAR DISTANCES

There is only one direct method of finding stellar distance – trigonometric parallax. In the introduction we found that parallax is the apparent shift of a star as the earth orbits the sun each year. The illustration below shows a diagram of how trigonometric parallax occurs. Notice that there is a very thin triangle with the small angle at a star. This angle is called the parallax angle,

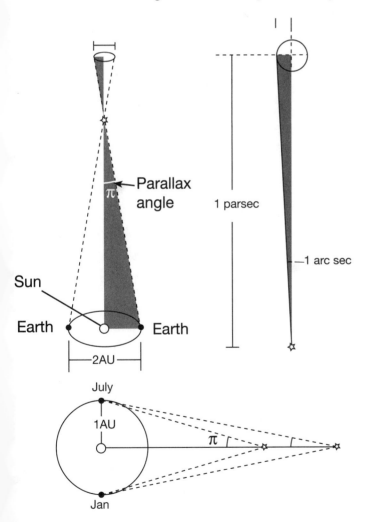

Trigonometric paralax

and is usually designated by the letter π. Here π is a variable, not the constant defined to be the ratio of a circle's circumference to its radius and approximated by 3.14. One leg of the triangle is the line between the star and the sun, and the other leg is the line between the star and the earth. The base of the triangle is the line between the earth and sun. The base has a length of one astronomical unit (AU). The length of either of the two legs is the distance to the star, d. Since the parallax angle is so small, we can use the small angle approximation,

$$\pi = 1/d$$

In conventional units, the parallax would be measured in radians and the distance would be expressed in AU. Since stars are so far away, all parallax angles would be very tiny and distances would be very large when expressed in the conventional units. Therefore, astronomers use their own units. Parallax angle is measured in seconds of arc, and so a new unit of distance must be defined. The new unit is defined to have a value of one when the parallax is one second of arc. We define this unit to be the parsec (pronounced par-seck, and abbreviated pc) from parallax of one second of arc. A parsec is equal to 3.26 light years. The closest star, α Centauri, has a parallax of 0.76 arc seconds, so its distance is about 1.3 parsecs.

The first parallax was measured in the 1830s, and for 160 years all parallax measurements were done in pretty much the same way. The classical techniques from the ground have errors of about 0.01 arc second. Since this error amounts to a parallax of 100 pc, many people mistakenly conclude that measurements by these methods will yield distances out to about 100 pc (or about 300 light years). However, when the error is the same size as the measurement, we cannot be sure that we are measuring any parallax at all. Classical measurements can produce distances within 20% accuracy only to about 20 pc (65 light years).

During the 1990s several new techniques were pioneered to measure more accurate parallax. The most successful of these was the HIPPARCOS satellite launched by the European Space Agency. The HIPPARCOS mission measured the distances of several hundred thousand stars, with an accuracy that exceeds that of classical techniques by an order of a magnitude. We now know the distances of stars to nearly 200 pc, about 600 light years. The importance of the HIPPARCOS results is that they allow calibration of other, indirect methods.

There are other methods of finding stellar distances, though those methods are not as important as they were before HIPPARCOS. We will discuss two related methods. We have previously mentioned pulsating variable stars. Pulsating variables regularly repeat their light variations over an interval called the period. If we plot measured magnitudes over the period, we get what is called a light curve. The average magnitude is the average of the maximum and minimum magnitudes. Pulsating stars have distinctive light curves that are usually marked by a rapid rise to maximum light followed by a more gradual decline toward minimum light.

One class of pulsating stars, the RR Lyrae stars, appear to be very similar to one another. They vary by less than a magnitude, and they have periods of oscillation of a few hours up to less than a day. Their most important feature is that they all have about the same absolute average magnitude, 0.6. RR Lyrae stars are easy to identify by their light curves, and once we realize that they have the same absolute average magnitude, and then we can use their observed average magnitude to find their distances. RR Lyrae stars are very common in a kind of star cluster called a globular cluster, so they are very useful in determining the distances of globular clusters.

Similar to the RR Lyrae stars, but much larger and brighter, are the Cepheid variables. Cepheid variables are giant and super-giant stars that have periods of anywhere from a few days to more than 50 days. They can vary over a few magnitudes. Early in the 20th century the astronomer Henrietta Leavitt discovered that the period of a Cepheid variable is directly related to the average absolute magnitude. That is, the brighter that a Cepheid is, the longer that it takes for the star to vary. A calibrated plot of this relationship is called the period-luminosity relation. From a Cepheid's light curve we can read off its period. The period-luminosity relation gives us the absolute average magnitude. The average magnitude of the light curve is the average-apparent magnitude. The distance can be found as before.

Since both RR Lyrae and Cepheid variables may be seen much farther than the 600-light-year limit of trigonometric parallax, they allow us the find distances beyond what parallax can produce. However, the RR Lyrae and Cepheid variable methods of finding distances are indirect in that they rely upon the assumption of the constancy of the average RR Lyrae magnitudes and the validity of the period-luminosity relation of Cepheids. Both of these assumptions appear warranted from observations. All the other methods of finding distances rely upon similar sorts of assumptions, often based upon some well-accepted physics. The result is that stellar distances are probably known to a few hundred or even thousand light years with great confidence.

EXTRA-GALACTIC DISTANCES

Most methods of finding stellar distances apply only to stars within our own galaxy, the Milky Way. However, many of these methods also work on two small satellite galaxies of the Milky Way, the Large and Small Magellanic Clouds. They are about 160,000 light years away. Beyond these systems the only method of stellar distance that works is the Cepheid variables. This method works for galaxies out to a few tens of millions of years because Cepheid variables are so bright. Generally when we talk about distances of other galaxies, we must develop other methods based upon "standard candles." A standard candle is a bright object for which we think that we know how bright it is, or in other words, we

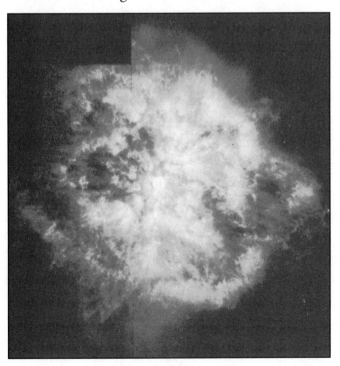

Supernova remnant

know its absolute magnitude. Examples of standard candles include bright globular clusters, HII (pronounced H-2) regions, super-giant stars, novae, and type Ia supernovae.

There are about 200 globular clusters in the Milky Way Galaxy. Since RR Lyrae stars are common in globular clusters, we have a good idea of how far away most of them are. Knowing their distances we can estimate how bright each cluster is and how large each cluster is by how bright and how large each cluster appears to us. Astronomers have found that globular clusters in our galaxy do not have a large range in size or brightness. The biggest and brightest are surprisingly uniform. Assuming that globular clusters in other galaxies similar to the Milky Way follow similar trends, we can estimate the distances of those other galaxies by how large and bright their globular clusters appear.

HII regions are clouds of glowing gas excited by the UV photons given off by bright, hot stars in their midst. There are many HII regions in the Milky Way and other similar galaxies. While there is a greater range in HII-region brightness and size than with globular clusters, the largest and brightest ones appear to be uniform from galaxy to galaxy. This uniformity allows us to treat the largest and brightest HII regions as standard candles.

Within a given galaxy of perhaps 200 billion stars, there will be a few dozen extremely bright stars. These are super-giant stars and represent the brightest stars of all. From galaxy to galaxy these bright super giants appear to have about the same absolute magnitude, so they too represent a standard candle. From time to time within galaxies there are novae (novae is plural, the singular is nova), stars that abruptly flare up in an eruption that lasts a few days. Astronomers think that novae are the result of material transferring from one star to another in a particular kind of binary-star system. The brightest novae all appear to have the about the same absolute magnitude, so they can be used as a standard candle as well. All of the standard candles mentioned thus far have nearly the same absolute magnitude, about –9. Generally, if more than one of these methods is available, all of the distance measurements are averaged.

A supernova is an extremely violent explosion of a star in which sometimes the precursor star is completely disrupted. A supernova may rival in brightness the galaxy in which it occurs. A supernova may remain near peak brightness for weeks before slowly fading over many months. There are two basic types of supernovae, type I and type II. The two types are markedly different in the types of light curves that they follow and the types of spectral lines that they have. A type II is the explosion of a very massive single star. Type II supernovae have considerable range in their peak brightness. Type I supernova result from mass transfer in close binary stars where the star that is gaining mass is a special kind of dense star, such as a white dwarf.

Of particular interest is a subset of type I supernovae, the type Ia. Type Ia supernovae have the same absolute magnitude near maximum light, about –19. Since we know the absolute magnitude of type Ia supernovae, we can use them to measure extremely large distances, often leapfrogging over other methods. A type Ia supernova occurs perhaps once or twice per century in any galaxy, so we can see a number of them per year in other galaxies. Type Ia

supernovae have been used to measure distances of galaxies more than a billion light years away.

The Hubble relation was discussed in chapter 1, so it will not be further described here. To use the Hubble relation, the Hubble constant must be determined. We do this by measuring the distances of as many galaxies as possible, and comparing the distances to the measured redshifts. The greatest difficulty is that nearby galaxies have the best distances, but the lowest redshifts, while more distant galaxies have the poorest distances and the greatest redshifts. A redshift is comprised of two parts: a Doppler shift due to motion and a Hubble flow due to universal expansion. For nearby galaxies expansion is minimal, so Doppler motion tends to dominate the redshift. With increasing distance, Doppler motions do not change, but the Hubble flow increases. Ideally, we would like to use the most distant objects possible to calibrate the Hubble constant, because then any Doppler motion can be ignored. The problem is that we can best measure distances for nearby objects, while distant galaxies are difficult to measure. Most disagreement over the value of the Hubble constant centers on how to handle this problem. Since type Ia supernovae skip over large distances, they have become very important in finding the value of the Hubble constant. When all is said and done, we find that with some exceptions, distance does scale with redshift. The most plausible interpretation of this fact is that the universe is expanding.

In this appendix we have attempted to show how astronomers can determine basic stellar properties. Modern astronomy allows us to find the distances, sizes, temperatures, and masses of stars. This is incredible, given how far stars are from us.

1. What are the two types of telescopes? How are they different?

2. How do we determine the size of a telescope? What are the advantages of a larger telescope?

3. What are two peculiarities of the magnitude system for measuring stellar brightness?

4. What are the seven basic stellar spectral types? What factor is responsible for the various spectral types?

5. What do we learn by studying binary stars?

6. What is the only direct method for finding distances to stars? How far out can we measure stellar distances with this method today?

7. Why can Cepheid variables be used to find distances?

8. Why can type Ia supernovae be used to find distances?

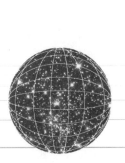

ENDNOTES

Chapter 1

1 A good discussion of the gap and day-age theories may be found in W.W. Fields, *Unformed and Unfilled* (Phillipsburg, NJ: Presbyterian and Reformed, 1978). A partial refutation of progressive creation may be found in M. Van Bebber and P.S. Taylor, *Creation and Time: A Report on the Progressive Creationist Book by Hugh Ross* (Gilbert, AZ: Eden Communications, 1994), or see H.M. Morris and J.D. Morris, *Science, Scripture, and the Young Earth* (El Cajon, CA: Institute for Creation Research, 1989), p. 7–10; or A.S. Kulikovsky, "God's Rest in Hebrews 4:1–11," *Creation Ex Nihilo Technical Journal* 13(2): 61–62 (1999). Theistic evolution has been critiqued in many places, such as H.M. Morris, *Scientific Creationism* (Green Forest, AR: Master Books, 1985), p. 215–220. A discussion of all of these compromising ideas may be found in D. Hall and J. Pipa, editors, *Did God Create in Six Days?* "From Chaos to Cosmos: A Critique of the Non-Literal Interpretations of Genesis 1:1–2:3," by J.A. Pipa (Taylors, SC: Southern Presbyterian Press, 1999), p. 153ff.

2 Some Christians go so far as to think that God gave Adam the complete story of redemption in the form of the constellation and star names that have been passed down to us, though garbled a bit. This idea has become known as the "gospel in the stars." For instance, see Frances Rolleston, *Mazzaroth* (York Beach, ME: Weiser Books, 2001), originally printed 1863; E.W. Bullinger, *Witness of the Stars* (Grand Rapids, MI: Kregel Publications, 1967), originally published 1893; J.A. Seiss, *The Gospel in the Stars* (Grand Rapids, MI: Kregel Publications, 1972), originally published 1882; or J. Kennedy, *The Real Meaning of the Zodiac* (Fort Lauderdale, FL: Coral Ridge Ministries, 1989). For a critical discussion of the gospel in the stars, see D.R. Faulkner, "Is There a Gospel in the Stars?" *Creation Ex Nihilo Technical Journal* 12(2): 169–172 (1998).

3 For a good refutation of the myth that the Medieval Church taught a flat earth, see J.B. Russell, *Inventing the Flat Earth* (New York: Praeger, 1991).

4 For a critical evaluation of modern geocentricism, see D.R. Faulkner, "Geocentricism and Creation," *Creation TJ* 15(2): 110–121 (2001).

Chapter 2

1 R.E. Walsh, editor, *The Fourth International Conference on Creationism,* by P.W. Dennis (Pittsburgh, PA: Creation Science Fellowship, 1998), p. 167–200.

2 D.R. Humphreys, *Creation and Time* (Green Forest, AR: Master Books, 1994).

Chapter 3

1 The definitive work on the anthropic principle is the one by Barrow and Tipler, *The Cosmological Anthropic Principle* (Oxford, England: Oxford University Press, 1988). Interestingly, Barrow and Tipler fully discuss the evidence for the anthropic principle before finally concluding that the universe merely appears designed.

2 See for instance, H. Ross, *The Fingerprint of God* (Orange, CA: Promise Publishing, 1989); or H. Ross, *The Creator and the Cosmos* (Colorado Springs, CO: Navpress, 1995). For a critical analysis of Hugh Ross's apologetics, see D.R. Faulkner, "The Dubious Apologetics of Hugh Ross," *Creation Ex Nihilo Technical Journal* 13(2): 52–60 (1999).

3 See, for instance, M. Rees, *Before the Beginning: Our Universe and Others* (Reading, MA: Helix Books: 1997).

4 H. Ross, *Beyond the Cosmos* (Colorado Springs, CO: Navpress, 1996). For reviews of this book, see W.L. Craig, *Journal of the Evangelical Theological Society* 24(2): 293–304 (1999), or D.R. Faulkner, *Creation Research Society Quarterly* 34:242–243 (1998).

Chapter 4

1 For a discussion of stellar population types, see D.R. Faulkner, "The Role of Stellar Population Types in the Discussion of Stellar Evolution" *Creation Research Society Quarterly* 30: 8–11 (1992).

2 R. Jastrow, *God and the Astronomers* (New York: W.W. Norton and Co., 1978).

3 See for instance, H. Ross, *The Fingerprint of God* (Orange, CA: Promise Publishing, 1989); or H. Ross, *The Creator and the Cosmos* (Colorado Springs, CO: Navpress, 1995).

4 Q. Smith, *British Journal for the Philosophy of Science* 45:649-668 (1994).

5 S. Weinberg, *The First Three Minutes* (New York: Basic Books, 1977).

6 M. Rees, *Before the Beginning: Our Universe and Others* (New York: Perseus Books Group, 1998).

7 P. Davies, *God and the New Physics* (New York: Simon and Schuster, 1983).

8 P. Davies, *The Mind of God* (New York: Simon and Schuster, 1992).

9 S. Hawking, *A Brief History of Time: From the Big Bang to Black Holes* (New York: Bantam, 1990).

Chapter 5

1 H. Arp, *Quasars, Redshifts, and Controversies* (Berkeley, CA: Interstellar Media, 1987), and *Seeing Red: Redshifts, Cosmology, and Academic Science* (Montreal, Canada: C. Roy Keys, Inc., 2002).

Chapter 6

1 E. Lerner, *The Big Bang Never Happened* (New York: Random House, 1991).

Chapter 7

1 Weston Fields, *Unformed and Unfilled* (Nutley, NJ: Presbyterian and Reformed Publishing Co., 1976).

2 H. Blocher, translated by D. Preston, *In the Beginning: The Opening Chapters of Genesis* (Leicester, England and Downer's Grove, IL: Inter-Varsity Press, 1984).

3 P. Stoner, *Science Speaks* (Chicago, IL: Moody Press, 1958).

4 J.K. West, *Creation Research Society Quarterly.*

5 A, Montgomery, "Third International Conference on Creationism," (Pittsburgh, PA: Creation Science Fellowship, 1994), p. 369.

6 For example, see the mini-symposium on this in the *CRSQ.*

7 D.R. Humphreys, *Starlight and Time* (Green Forest, AR: Master Books, 1994).

8 P. Moon and D.E. Spencer, "Binary Stars and the Velocity of Light," *Journal of the Optical Society of America* 43(8): 635–641 (1953).

Chapter 8

1 R.E. Walsh, editor, "The Current State of Creation Astronomy" by D.R. Faulkner, *The Fourth International Conference on Creationism* (1998) p. 201–216.

2 D.R. Faulkner, "A Biblically Based Cratering Theory," *Creation Ex Nihilo.*

3 D.R. Faulkner, *Impact 300.*

Appendix

1 Wayne Spencer, *TJ.*

ANSWERS TO CHAPTER QUESTIONS

Introduction

1. Cosmology is the study of the structure of the universe. Cosmogony is the study of the history of the universe.

2. The ancients used several proofs to show that the earth was spherical. One proof was the fact that the earth's shadow during a lunar eclipse is always round. Another proof is that the position of the visible stars changed as one traveled northward or southward.

3. Eratosthenes measured the size of the earth 22 centuries ago. He did this by measuring the different angles of the sun at noon on the same date at different latitudes.

4. The geocentric model is the theory that the earth is the center of the universe with the sun and other planets orbiting the earth.

5. Copernicus published a book that argued for the heliocentric theory. In his book, he found the orbital periods of the planets and determined the relative sizes of the planets.

6. The Tychonic model was a compromise cosmology, where the other planets orbited the sun, but the sun in turn orbited the earth each year.

7. Galileo saw that the moon was imperfect in that it had mountains and craters. He saw spots on the sun, which made that body

imperfect as well. Galileo saw Venus go through phases, which meant that that body orbited the sun. He saw satellites orbiting Jupiter, objects that the ancients did not know about and obviously orbited something other than the earth. Lastly, Galileo saw many other stars too faint to be seen with the naked eye.

8. William Herschel was the first to determine the basic shape of our galaxy in his grindstone model.

9. The island universe theory is the idea that our galaxy is just one of many galaxies. The opposite viewpoint was that there are no other galaxies beside our Milky Way galaxy.

Chapter 1

1. The two pillars of modern physics are quantum mechanics and general relativity.

2. In Newtonian physics, gravity acts at a distance through empty space with no known mechanism. In general relativity, gravity is transmitted through space by curving space.

3. The first confirmation for general relativity was the bending of starlight around the sun observed in the 1919 total solar eclipse.

4. A static universe is a universe that is neither expanding nor contracting.

5. The cosmological constant was a repulsive term that Einstein introduced into his cosmology to produce a static universe.

6. Homogeneity means that the universe has the same properties everywhere.

7. Isotropy means that the universe has the same properties or appearance in every direction.

8. The cosmological principle is the assumption that the universe is both homogeneous and isotropic. The cosmological principle usually leads to the big-bang model.

9. The perfect cosmological principle is the assumption that the universe is both homogeneous and isotropic at all times. The cosmological principle usually leads to the steady-state, or continuous creation, model.

10. The cosmic background radiation (CBR) was predicted by the big-bang model, so the CBR is the best evidence for the big-bang theory. On the other hand, the steady state does not predict the CBR, so most cosmologists think that the CBR disproves the steady-state theory.

11. The expansion of the universe and the abundances of the light elements do not constitute proof of the big bang model, because those data were inputs into the big-bang model. That is, these are examples of explanatory power, not predictive power.

12. A bound universe is a universe that has an edge or boundary.

Chapter 2

1. The flatness problem is the question of why the value of Ω is so close to 1. With time, the value of Ω ought to rapidly depart from 1, so the value of Ω initially had to be extremely close to 1. Only in a universe with Ω near 1 is life possible, so the universe appears contrived. This is called the flatness problem, because a universe with Ω equal to 1, the universe has no curvature.

2. The anthropic principle is the principle that the universe appears designed for our existence.

3. Inflation is the idea that very early in time the universe rapidly expanded faster than the speed of light. Inflation was devised to explain the flatness problem, but it also attempts to explain other questions, such as why the universe has a homogeneous temperature (the horizon problem).

4. Dark matter is invisible mass whose existence is demanded by the gravitational forces that the dark matter apparently exerts. Unlike "normal" matter, dark matter gives off no light.

5. The COBE and WMAP missions found slight temperature variations in the CBR. These variations are required by the big-bang model, but the actual temperature variations were below the level initially predicted by the big bang.

6. Dark energy is a force causing the expansion of the universe to accelerate, which is opposite to the effect that matter has. Dark energy is very similar to Einstein's old cosmological constant.

7. The Hubble time is the reciprocal of the Hubble constant, and it is the rough age of the universe in the big-bang model.

8. Cosmologists have suggested that the universe began as a quantum fluctuation out of nothing or in another, pre-existing universe. Other cosmologists have suggested that the universe is oscillating between big bangs and "big crunches." Some cosmologists have suggested that the universe is infinite and that it always has expanded from much higher energy states and will continue to do so.

Chapter 3

1. The redshifts of galaxies are not the result of the Doppler effect, but are due to Hubble flow, the expansion of space between the galaxies.

2. If a galaxy is nearby, and if its local motion due to gravity is toward us and exceeds the galaxy's feeble Hubble flow, then that galaxy can have a blueshift, rather than a redshift.

3. The twin paradox results from a misunderstanding of modern relativity theory. Consider identical twins, with one twin taking a

space trip at nearly the speed of light while the other remains on earth. Because of time dilation, one twin ages very little, while the other twin ages a great deal. If all reference frames are equal, then who is to say which twin is actually moving and thus which twin ages very little? The resolution of the twin paradox is the realization that not all reference frames are equal. According to Mach's principle, the twin on the earth remains most at rest with respect to the total of the mass of the universe, so his frame of reference is preferred over his brother's. Therefore, the twin aboard the space ship is the one doing the moving.

4. Modern relativity theory does not allow for material objects to travel faster than the speed of light, because that would require infinite energy. However, as the universe expands, particles in the universe are usually nearly at rest with respect to space. It is space itself that is expanding faster than the speed of light, not the particles.

5. Unless a galaxy's redshift is very large, that galaxy will not appear redder than normal. Even a high redshift galaxy appears only slightly redder. It is the spectral lines that are shifted, not the overall color.

6. The speed of light in a vacuum is about 300,000 km/s. In matter, such as air, glass, or water, the speed of light is always less than what it is in a vacuum. The constancy of the speed of light refers to the fact that whenever we measure the speed of light, its value is always independent of our motion. If we move toward or away from a source of light, the speed that we measure is always 300,000 km/s.

7. The name "big-bang" suggests that the universe began as an explosion, and explosions are always random, chaotic events. Actually the big-bang model posits that the universe came into existence in a highly ordered expanding state.

8. This is an improper question, because according the big-bang theory, the big bang was the first event in time, so there was no such thing as, "before the big bang." Furthermore, the question also suggest that space existed before the big bang, but in the big-bang model, space came into existence when the rest of the universe did.

Chapter 4

1. Most astronomers think that quasars are very massive black holes at great distances. According to this theory, they produce great luminosity by way of in-falling matter. Quasars may be the cores of distant galaxies.

2. Halton Arp has argued that quasar redshifts are not cosmological, so that quasars are actually very close to us. To support his contention, Arp has presented evidence that calls into question how reliable the assumption of cosmological redshifts is.

3. Some astronomers think that redshifts of galaxies tend to clump around certain values, such as 72 km/sec. This is difficult to explain in the big-bang model.

4. The COBE experiment was designed to measure slight temperature variations in the CBR predicted by the big-bang model. The measured temperature variations were an order of magnitude less than predicted. The big-bang model was recalculated to produce the observed temperature variations.

5. No, all observations strongly suggest that the universe is not homogeneous. It is an assumption that at some high level the universe is uniform.

Chapter 5

1. Modern cosmological theories require that the universe be homogeneous, but the fact that we appear to be in a very large quasar-free region of space violates this assumption. The steady-state theory cannot explain this.

2. Unlike the steady state theory, in the big-bang model the universe and the objects in it are evolving and aging. If the universe is more than 10 billion years old and quasars are galaxies in their infancy, then there shouldn't be infant galaxies anymore.
We would see infant galaxies only at great distances where it has taken their light billions of years to reach us.

3. The second law of thermodynamics states that energy becomes less useful with time. If the universe has always existed, as the steady state theory claims, then there would have been more than enough time for the energy in the universe to become totally useless, or at maximum entropy. This is not what we observe.

4. Unlike other cosmological models that assume gravity is the dominant force controlling the overall structure of the universe, the plasma model assumes that electromagnetic forces are the primary forces shaping the universe.

Chapter 6

1. The day-age theory is the belief that the days of the creation week were long periods of time.

2. The framework hypothesis is the belief that since the first few chapters of Genesis contain poetic elements that these passages are poetry and need not be taken as historical narrative.

3. Evolution is a purely natural, purely physical explanation of our existence and the existence of the world.

4. Some creationists question whether the universe is expanding in an attempt to undermine the big-bang theory. They reason that if the universe is not expanding, then the big bang cannot be true. This is correct, but the big bang is not the only possible cosmological model based upon universal expansion. If we reject universal expansion, it may prevent us from discovering a creation-based cosmology.

5. The translators of the Septuagint translated Genesis to reflect the cosmology current in their day – that the heavens consisted of a hard, transparent sphere. In similar fashion, modern Christians who accept the big bang interpret Genesis in terms of the dominant cosmology of our day.

6. The universe appears to be billions of light years across. The light-travel-time problem is the question of how light from much of the universe could have reached the earth if the universe is only thousands of years old, as most creationists believe. Creationists have offered several explanations.

7. A white hole is a region of space packed with a large amount of matter into a high density so that its gravity is very large. A white hole is very similar to a black hole, except that matter and energy stream out of a white hole and into a black hole.

8. Most theorists doubt that white holes exist today because of two reasons. First, there is no known natural explanation of how a white hole could form. Second, white holes are very unstable and thus evaporate very quickly.

Chapter 7

1. There are two reasons why progress in developing a creation model has been so slow. One reason is that there are so few qualified researchers in the field. The other reason is that we have so few biblical specifics about astronomy and creation.

2. The word *raqia* means something that is beaten out, as one might beat or stretch out a metal into a sheet. Elsewhere, the Bible mentions that God stretched out the heavens. This is very similar to the modern cosmological idea of the expanding universe.

3. In the Bible, a star is any luminous star-like object in the sky. By their appearance, modern day aircraft at night would fit this definition.

4. Romans 8:22 suggests that all of the universe shared in the curse as a result of man's sin.

5. If we attach the big bang too closely to our understanding of creation in Genesis, then when that theory is discarded, our understanding of Genesis must be discarded as well. In the minds of many, this would discredit the Genesis creation account as well.

Appendix

1. The two types of telescopes are the refractor and reflector. A refracting telescope uses a large lens to form the image, while a reflecting telescope uses a large curved mirror to form the image.

2. The size of a telescope is determined by the diameter of its objective (the lens or mirror). A larger telescope gathers more light, allowing us to see fainter and more distant objects. A larger telescope also produces better resolution, which means that we see more detail in the image.

3. One peculiarity of the magnitude system is that the system runs backward – the greater the number, the fainter the star. The other peculiarity is that the system is logarithmic, which means the differences in brightness are compressed numerically.

4. The spectral types are O, B, A, F, G, K, and M. This order corresponds to decreasing temperature.

5. The study of a binary star tells us the masses of the stars in the system.

6. The only direct method for finding stellar distances is trigonometric parallax. The HIPPARCOS mission allowed us to measure distances out to about 200 pc (600 light years) with this method.

7. We can use Cepheid variables to find distances, because Cepheids follow a period-luminosity relation. That is, the brightest Cepheid variables have the longest periods. Therefore, if we measure a Cepheid's period, we know how bright it is, and so we can compute its distance by comparing its actual brightness to how bright it appears to us.

INDEX

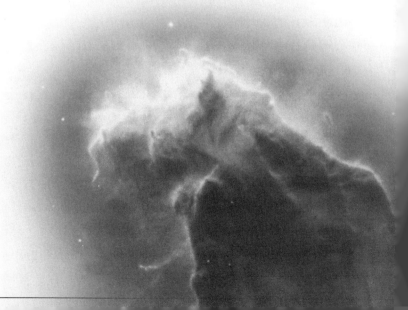

BODY BY DESIGN

ALAN L. GILLEN

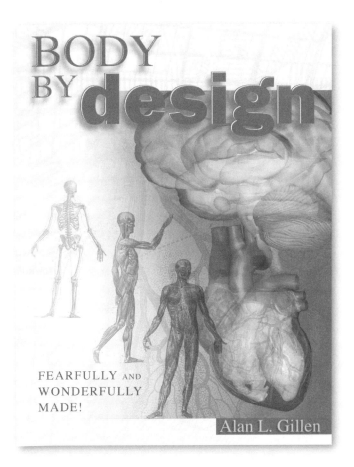

Body by Design defines the basic anatomy and physiology in each of 11 body systems from a creational viewpoint. Each chapter

- Explores the wonder, beauty and creation of the human body
- Gives evidence for creation
- Exposes faulty evolutionistic reasoning
- Looks closely at disease aspects, current events and discoveries
- Profiles the classic and contemporary scientists and physicians who have made remarkable breakthroughs in studies of the different areas of the human body.

Body by Design is an ideal textbook for Christian high school or college students as it utilizes tables, graphs, focus sections, diagrams, and illustrations to provide clear examples and explanations of the ideas presented. Questions at the end of each chapter challenge the student to think through the evidence

$13.99
ISBN 0-89051-296-5 • 160 pages • 8-1/2 x 11 paperback

Available at Christian bookstores nationwide
Find other great titles at www.masterbooks.net